JUST WRITE
HERE'S HOW

Shooter

The Dream Bearer

Handbook for Boys: A Novel

Patrol: An American Soldier in Vietnam
Illustrated by Ann Grifalconi

Bad Boy: A Memoir

Malcolm X: A Fire Burning Brightly
Illustrated by Leonard Jenkins

Monster

Angel to Angel: A Mother's Gift of Love

Glorious Angels: A Celebration of Children

The Story of the Three Kingdoms
Illustrated by Ashley Bryan

Brown Angels: An Album of Pictures and Verse

The Righteous Revenge of Artemis Bonner

Now Is Your Time!:
The African-American Struggle for Freedom

The Mouse Rap

Scorpions

Tales of a Dead King

JUST WRITE
HERE'S HOW

WALTER DEAN MYERS

Collins

An Imprint of HarperCollinsPublishers

Portions of this book have previously appeared in somewhat different form in interviews, journals, magazines, and lectures, including the American Library Association's *Children and Libraries*, ALA *Booklist*, *Book Report*, the *Knoxville News Sentinel*, NPR, *Publishers Weekly*, *School Library Journal*, and VOYA.

Collins is an imprint of HarperCollins Publishers.

Library of Congress catalog card number: 2012931468
ISBN 978-0-06-220389-2 (trade bdg.) — ISBN 978-0-06-220390-8 (pbk.)

Typography by Carla Weise
12 13 14 15 16 LP/RRDH 10 9 8 7 6 5 4 3 2 1
❖
First Edition

Contents

PROLOGUE: Why I'm a Writer 1

CHAPTER 1: Roll Up Your Sleeves 15

CHAPTER 2: Something Old, Something New, Something
Borrowed, Something Blue 26

CHAPTER 3: Hello, Voices in My Head 40

CHAPTER 4: Map It Out 45

CHAPTER 5: Lights, Camera, Action! 53

CHAPTER 6: Nice to Meet You 62

CHAPTER 7: What's Going On? 68

CHAPTER 8: Where's the Fire? 71

CHAPTER 9: What's It to You? 75

CHAPTER 10: Get It Together 80

CHAPTER 11: So What Are You Going to Do About It? 84

CHAPTER 12: Then What Happened? 87

CHAPTER 13: For Real? 89

CHAPTER 14: Check It Out 97

CHAPTER 15: Discipline 105

CHAPTER 16: Leave Your Ego at the Door 109

CHAPTER 17: Hey, Get Back Here 113

CHAPTER 18: There's Room on This Page for the Both of Us ..117

CHAPTER 19: Pick Yourself Up, Dust Yourself Off 121

CHAPTER 20: Writing Is Good for You 124

CHAPTER 21: Who Are You? 126

AFTERWORD: Now You're a Writer

                    By Ross Workman 133

TOP TEN WRITING TIPS FROM WALTER DEAN MYERS...................... 143

FIVE WRITING TIPS FROM ROSS WORKMAN 145

SUGGESTIONS FOR FURTHER READING 147

MEET THE AUTHOR 149

ALL MY BOOKS ... SO FAR 155

JUST WRITE
HERE'S HOW

WHY I'M A WRITER

I love what I do.

After forty-three years and over one hundred books, it still amazes me that I have been lucky enough to spend most of my life doing what I truly love: writing. That people read what I write, that I have won awards for my writing, and that I have been able to make a living at it are extras for which I am very grateful. Success at writing simply means that I am able to continue to write instead of having to get some other job. The many returns my readers have given me for my efforts have exceeded my most ambitious expectations.

I care about writing for young people because I

1

remember how much I needed help and guidance at that time in my life. My own life showed me the value of stories, and I've spent my career trying to write the books I wanted to read as a teen.

Books and writing have always been a part of my life. There is no substitute for reading. There are two elements I recognize as reading: "decoding" the letters or symbols that form words and phrases (what you learned to do when you were first beginning to recognize letters and sound out words), and the transition from the decoding process to "ownership" of the text (what you probably felt the first time you read a book you really loved).

I was lucky to experience ownership at an early age. I'll just tell you right up front that I was a mama's boy. My happiest memories of my childhood are of spending time with my mother, Florence Dean, in our small Harlem apartment. There I first encountered stories. Mama and I would listen to her radio shows or she would read out loud to me. Then we would discuss the stories together and share what they meant to us. You probably do this in English class at school, or maybe with your friends. "Ownership" is when you really get into a book or a movie (or a video game), and you almost feel like it's happening to you. You know it's not *really* happening, of course—but the characters' emotions feel real, and maybe you can imagine being part of the story yourself. Have you ever felt this way about a story?

In my conversations at home with my mother, I became used to transferring information from one person to another and to the imaginative process involved. Long before I started school, I was "reading ready" and only had to worry about expanding the decoding process.

I defined decoding just above as the mechanical process of reading, of recognizing letters and the sounds they make, and knowing what the words mean. These are the building blocks, but decoding involves more than just phonics or knowing the dictionary definitions of lots of different words. There's a deeper aspect of understanding a story. Have you ever read a story in school that took place at another time in history, such as during the Vietnam War? Your teacher might have thought it was important to study a little bit about the Vietnam War to give you context to understand the story even better. Or maybe you've read a story about a character who is very different from you— maybe from another country with a unique culture. Being able to understand that character's perspective is also part of the decoding process. There are a lot of ways to get better and better at decoding. The more you learn throughout your life, whether through reading, exploring, or experiencing new things, the greater your capacity for understanding will become.

In many ways, I had a head start in decoding as well as in ownership. I got to travel around New York City with my church, gaining exposure to many different places and cultures. This made me more comfortable with the new ideas I would find in books. I had a relatively wide range of intellectual experiences, even at age seven, that served me well.

My transition from being a reader to being a writer happened naturally. I liked to read and I liked to be sociable, but I tended to fight a lot in school, which limited my social network. The fighting often stemmed from my speech problems. The frustration I felt as I rattled off my ideas to bewildered teachers and fellow students often ended up with me punching someone. I was frequently admonished for "not playing well with others." The problem was that the "others" didn't always do what I told them to do.

When I'm writing I create my own "others," my characters, and I play very well with them. I went from creating another world in my head to doing it on paper.

The discipline of forming the details that made up a poem or story was one I enjoyed immensely.

I'm often asked why I write for young people. My own experiences as a teenager were so intense that I keep coming back to that period of my life to explore and to make sense of it in a way that defines who I am today. I've used my own experiences to understand the characters I write about. What I do is fairly simple. I write books for the troubled boy I once was, and for the boy who lives within me still.

Why do I revisit that time in my life through writing? Why not through psychotherapy or interpretive dance? I think the answer has something to do with the power of the written word. I believe in that power deeply. Through literature, the reader and the writer are provided with a vehicle for direct communication. Every individual is unique, but through writing we can reach out and, hopefully, meet somewhere in the middle. We can understand a person we have never met and know a place we've never seen.

Maybe even more important than transporting us to faraway places, reading and writing can also bring us closer to our own inner selves. As we identify and empathize with other people, we reaffirm our own abilities to make that human connection. We remember we're not really that different. There are elements of the experience of living that we all share.

Life is imperfect and often complicated. (If your life is perfect, congratulations. Seriously.) Usually the reason for the complication has to do with other people. When kids used to make fun of me when I had to read out loud in class, they were laughing because that's what they wanted to do. When I punched them, that was what I wanted to do. If we went around doing whatever we wanted, the world would be sort of a mess. So outside of what I want and outside of what you want, we've agreed on some things that we *all* want. Some people call this morality, or the social contract, even common sense, but somehow we manage to get along with each other.

Stories allow us to think about all this. We can explore how we would react to certain situations without actually having to live through them. We can imagine how we would feel and think about what we would do and whether we agree or disagree with a character's decisions and actions. We can fine-tune our own definitions of right and wrong.

It's a gift to be able to go outside our own limited worlds in this way. That gift was given to me. Reading probably saved my life. In some ways, I mean that figuratively, because the ideas I found in books helped me imagine a life I wanted to live. If I wasn't a reader, I would have missed out on a lot of the things I've come to consider meaningful.

But reading also literally saved my life.

We each are born into a history. We have a mother and a father; we have certain physical features and are born in a specific place. As writers, we get to invent different histories for our characters. To do this skillfully, we must seek to more deeply understand our own individual histories and their effect on us.

I was born in Martinsburg, West Virginia. I was named Walter Milton Myers. My family (I don't actually remember any of this!) was relatively poor. It is not surprising that, when my mother died two years later, I was taken in by family friends, Herbert and Florence Dean. The Deans lived in a busy section of Harlem, New York, which would later become a setting for many of my stories. My living with them meant that I was taken away from my brothers and sisters, who remained in West Virginia.

Losing my family was unfortunate, but in other ways I was incredibly lucky. The Harlem of my youth was a cultural and creative hub. My difficulties in school often led me to my local library branch or to the solitude of my room, where I developed a deep love of reading and the written word. My parents—though not perfect—loved me and encouraged me in my intellectual pursuits.

When I visit juvenile detention facilities, I ask myself: "Why not me?" I didn't have the easiest time as a teenager. I dropped out of high school and narrowly escaped arrest. I left home on a Friday, the twentieth of August 1954, to join the army. A few days later, the police came looking for me at my parents' apartment.

Somehow, things turned around for me. I think a lot about how, and why. Maybe if I can figure out what went right, I'll be able to help some of the young people who no doubt feel the same despair I did. Certainly some of it was luck: being given as a toddler to loving foster parents, being raised in Harlem at a time in history when a rich culture existed there, even the police showing up after I'd left home. My characters, and many real-life young people, are not so lucky. I worry about these kids because I often think about my personal history and marvel at how easily things could have turned out differently.

Growing up, I made assumptions about the world, as all kids do, based on my immediate surroundings. I also made assumptions about myself. What I understood first was that I was black and poor. My adult role models were my father, who was a janitor, and my mother, who cleaned apartments.

I had a happy childhood for the most part, but I remember beginning to feel despair as I became a teenager. There wasn't one specific thing that happened. It was a combination of bad things. When I was fourteen, my uncle was murdered. The brutal death of his brother sent my father spiraling into a deep depression during which he wouldn't leave his room for days. My mother, who had always struggled with alcoholism, began to drink more heavily. Sometime around then, I started to understand that even though I was good at school and loved to read, college wouldn't be a possibility for me. My family could barely afford to keep me in high school. I had been working after school since I was fourteen but made just enough money for lunch and taking the subway.

Until I was a teen, I didn't really understand that being poor could limit what I could do. I didn't want to end up like my uncle or my mother, but I wasn't sure what the alternative could be. I stopped caring about school. The limitations that I felt the world was putting on me made me angry. By the time I was fifteen, I was getting in trouble regularly and had to report to a city agency once a week for supervision.

I speak with thousands of young people around the country each year in middle schools, high schools, and juvenile detention centers. When we talk, I recognize in their lives similar moments to my own life. You might recall being asked as a child what you would like to be when you grow up. When you're very young, growing up is something that *will* happen to you sometime in the future. Then there's an almost imperceptible shift. All of a sudden, at some point, life stops being something that will happen to you and, instead, starts just happening. This is when reality sets in.

You look at the world around you and internalize it. You think of the world as being a part of you and see yourself as having a place in it. If the world around you happens to be a good place, you're a very fortunate person. For me, and for many teens, the world around me was not a good place. The process of becoming a part of the world around me and the prospect of taking a place in that world made me lose hope. I didn't know how I could overcome my circumstances, which looked bleak and very different from the idea of success my parents and teachers had given me as a child.

There was one place in my world that saved me from complete despair. The George Bruce Branch of the New York Public Library on West 125th Street became my home away from home, allowing me to escape the chaotic world around me. I could enter the library and participate fully, despite empty pockets. In the library stacks I could immerse myself in André Gide or Honoré de Balzac or Ernest Hemingway, and join a universe that would otherwise be denied me. There was no way I could have afforded to buy the books.

My circumstances often seemed insurmountable to me, but through reading I reached out for ideas that might help me escape them. The books I read showed me options other than those I saw reflected in my surroundings. They gave me new definitions for success in my life.

After the army, I held a series of low-paying jobs at a factory, a mailroom, a post office. I ended up working in construction, and was having a particularly trying day when I remembered something a high school teacher had said to me years earlier: "Whatever you do, don't stop writing." That afternoon, on my way home after work, I bought a composition notebook. I started writing in it and felt more alive right away.

I sent my poems, short stories, and some longer pieces out to publishing houses and received rejection after rejection. But I kept at it. I noticed that even though I didn't have a college degree (I hadn't even technically graduated from high school), I was able to get better and better jobs because of my reading and writing skills. Eventually, I entered a story in a contest run by the Council on Interracial Books for Children. My entry, *Where Does the Day Go?*, became my first published book.

What my experience has shown me is that the books I read, along with my love of reading and writing, were my way of dealing with the despair I often felt. When I heard the world and my own voice in my ear, telling me I wasn't good enough, the alternative life I found in books—reading them and writing them—kept some of my self-esteem intact. They made me believe I could have a different sort of life than that of the adults I knew. The early poems and stories I wrote were my entree into a much more comfortable world.

It wasn't until years after my painful adolescence that I started writing regularly, and it wasn't until years later that I began to make a living as a writer. But I see my success today as stemming from those moments spent lost in the world of a book, seeking hope at a time when I felt most vulnerable.

I'm not sure why I remember this part of my life so

vividly, but I do. It's why I love creating teenage characters, exploring how their inner lives and experiences reflect my own or differ from them. It's why I love having an open dialogue with young people. It's why I love writing for young people. There were books that helped me see an alternative, and I like to believe that I now write that kind of book.

I had a lot of chances to go down a bad path as a teenager, but instead I went to the library. The world inside my head was richly furnished with ideas I got from books, and it provided an escape from the dangerous world around me.

Books saved my life, so I know it is at least possible for a book to perform that feat. I realize this probably happens quite infrequently. When I think about all the books that are written and published in the world, it seems even more unlikely that one of *my* books could end up in a position to do such a thing. I like to believe that my books will at least provide some entertainment. So, just in case, I keep on writing and writing.

What I do in my work time is write. What I do in my spare time varies but often involves either reading or writing.

I tell the young people I meet to read. Read everything you can, looking for the ideas that give you hope and expand your sense of what's possible. If you can't find something you're looking for in a book, write it yourself. Try to get published. You have stories that other kids might need to read. You have stories that should be heard. Maybe a reader will find your book when the timing's just right and it will help save a life. So just write.

CHAPTER 1

Roll Up Your Sleeves

Some authors pretend that writing is easy. Maybe it's fun for them to imagine they are very special, enlightened beings who sit still and wait quietly for inspiration. Maybe it really is easy for some people. I don't know. For me and for the young people I have written with and mentored, it is work. Hopefully it will be fun work for you. If you find the nuts and bolts of writing—the thinking and the revision processes—to be fun, that means you're a writer.

I don't necessarily think I am particularly talented. I do think I am a successful writer. This is because of my work ethic and the discipline that's allowed me to create a useful structure for myself that helps me through the writing process.

The structure is simply a question or problem, a logical road leading to an answer to that question or problem, and the answer or conclusion itself. We can make this even simpler by calling it a "beginning" (question or problem), a "middle" (the journey toward an ending), and an "end" (how the question or problem is resolved). If I am sure of the question or problem, and reasonably sure of the answer or solution, I have a good structure.

Writing is not mysterious. There are tools that I use to help me get to the end of a book. I want to share those tools with you so you can learn how to finish what you start. With these tools and a willingness to do the hard work of writing, you will be able to get to the end of a poem or a story or even a book.

This is what works for me, and what I've seen work for other teen authors I've mentored. Here's why I'm qualified to give advice. In addition to writing more than one hundred books, I've taught writing to high school and middle school students, visited young people in schools, libraries, and juvenile detention centers, and coauthored a published novel, *Kick*, with teen writer Ross Workman.

Over the years, I have been approached by many would-be writers like you. All kids are smart. Most are also thoughtful and interesting. They have wonderful ideas that I encourage them to explore and develop. I often offer to help guide them through the writing process, even to cowrite with them or show them what I think needs to be done. But even if they're thoughtful and interesting and I'm willing to help, it doesn't always work out. When it does work out, it's because the writer understands that writing is sometimes hard, and is enthusiastic about the writing process.

What do I mean by "the writing process," exactly? A process is a series of steps that are followed, a system, a method of production. A book doesn't just appear out of nowhere. Unfortunately, scientists haven't come up with a better way to turn thoughts into words, sentences, paragraphs, or chapters than good old-fashioned writing. It's fun and exciting to think up ideas, but that's not where the writing ends. That's barely even where it begins. Writing is a sometimes joyous, sometimes difficult trek through words, sentences, pages, and chapters. It is no task for the fainthearted.

First, I do a lot of thinking and prewriting. Prewriting is my way of testing an idea. I start with a brief and simple outline and then, slowly, begin to flesh it out. Since I write in the mornings at home, I often take the outline to the park or sometimes on the subway. If the idea is going to work, the outlining should be interesting, even fun. If it feels like drudgery and you're bored with your idea before you've even started writing, you can probably figure out that the idea isn't good enough to sustain a story from beginning to end.

This definitely happens to me quite frequently. I'm always glad I took the time to consider the idea before getting lost in the first few pages. It also helps maintain my confidence as a writer. I don't want to feel frustrated while I'm writing, because that makes me feel bad about myself. Those are the times when you might start to think you can't do it or you're not good enough.

By prewriting, I'm able to diagnose the flaws in my initial idea and figure out how I need to change my idea to make it more structurally sound. By thinking ahead of time, when you're doing the outline, you can diagnose many flaws in the initial idea and figure out what changes to make.

An example of this is when I wrote *The Legend of Tarik*. My main character's village was attacked by an evil dude, and the story begins with him being nursed back to health. The story was going to be about how

Tarik avenged the wrongs done to him and his village. After he is trained to use a sword, he sets off on his mission. But I quickly realized that he is going by himself, so he has no one to talk to about his intentions.

I redid the outline, adding a young girl warrior, Stria, so my hero could engage with her. She became a very interesting character. If you can make it to the end of an outline, you'll have the confidence of knowing that your idea and the plot will keep you and a reader interested.

I also make a plan before I start typing, because I've done this a few times before and I know how hard it's going to get. It's inevitable that at some point I'm going to find myself mired in the middle of a paragraph. If I make an outline, I'll have a life jacket I can hang on to and keep myself afloat. I've seen manuscripts abandoned halfway—my own and those of others—because the writer got lost. If I have a plan, hopefully it will help me stay on track as I forge through the writing process.

Where I've seen most writers fail is at this very early planning stage. They have a great idea but don't want to do the work to think it through. Once they start writing, they might find it exhilarating initially, but when it starts to get tougher, they don't have any support. They give up.

I've failed, too. Okay, so sometimes I'm so excited about an idea, I will plunge right in and start the story with no plan or outline. But then, when I find myself in trouble, I end up throwing away pages, if not whole chapters. Finishing the first draft becomes a lot harder. There are writers who tell me that they never know where a book is going, and that characters often "surprise" them. Usually these writers take a lot longer to complete their work than I do. My characters never "surprise" me. But as I learn more about them as I go along, I might have to change the outline and the story. And that's fine.

I think a lot more writers would successfully complete their books if they spent more time planning. I don't mean months or years of planning, but at least getting down the basic idea of where they're going and how they want to get there.

Some of my ideas have fallen through the cracks. I certainly haven't turned every idea I've ever had into a book. But I have turned some of my ideas into books. I know that you, too, might be able to, because I have seen at least one teen writer use my writing process to complete a manuscript that became a published novel.

It started in 2007, when Ross Workman, a middle

school student, sent me a fan email. He said he liked my writing and mentioned that he would like to be a writer one day. You can probably guess what I was thinking, based on how most of my attempts to work with teen writers had gone in the past, but I always give new writers a chance. My expectations were low. I suggested we outline a story idea—usually a turnoff for the young writer—and he agreed. We exchanged emails, knocking around story ideas, and settled on a plot using the background he had given me: He was a soccer player.

I was impressed that he kept responding. Okay, I thought, the kid seems serious. Let's see what he's got. I wrote a first chapter and emailed it to him. A week later, I opened my email and saw a message with an attachment. The young man, Ross, had written a chapter. It wasn't a great chapter, but he had done the work. I explained how I outlined books, and together we made an outline and created the characters. Ross thought the names I chose were old-fashioned, and we changed them. We both made adjustments to the outline and did some research before we actually started writing. I was impressed when Ross researched some of the legal aspects of the mystery. We had started the book with a complex problem, and my chapter took the viewpoint of an older black man looking at the dilemma. Ross's chapter took the viewpoint of a student who is, perhaps, in very deep trouble. Ross had to imagine the setting (he's never actually been arrested), but he moved the story along nicely.

Where was I going with this? The writer in me couldn't resist writing another chapter. So I did, and sent it off. A week later, Ross responded with *his* chapter. We were on our way. But how would Ross react to criticism? When I thought a chapter needed revision, I told him why I didn't care for it and what he would need to do to improve it.

I was quick to criticize Ross's efforts, but I was not going to write his chapters for him. I've had at least fifty people approach me wanting to "collaborate" on a book. What they usually mean is that they will supply the brilliant idea and I will merely do the drudge work of writing the book. I am not about to allow that to happen.

Ross seemed to understand that writing was work, and he was able to accept criticism. He seemed less willing to criticize my work, but he pointed out plot inaccuracies and character inconsistencies and would give me subtle hints when he felt I needed them.

Over the next weeks, we continued trading chapters,

and the story moved along more or less according to our outline. I was enjoying the collaboration.

I wasn't seriously considering publishing the book. I was simply showing a young person how a book is put together. There was no rah-rah, there were no inspirational talks, just writing technique. Write, write, rewrite, change what needs to be changed, even if you initially think it was good, then write some more.

When we were well into the book, I told my editor what I was doing and how much I was learning from the process. I couldn't wait to finish writing the book with Ross.

We finished a first draft and Ross was enthusiastic about the revisions, always a good sign. I showed our efforts to my editor. She had reservations. This didn't bother me at all, because it's part of the writing process. She also had some ideas for revisions. I thought her ideas were good but wondered how Ross would react.

Ross was still game and willing to do the revisions. I was surprised. I've had young people actually ask me to rewrite *their* manuscripts (promising me a cut of the profits!), and one nineteen-year-old told me that he didn't write his poetry at all, he rapped it. I could make a recording of it and type it up and market it for him if that was what I wanted to do.

I wanted to see if Ross would want to participate in the revision phase of the writing process. This was a different kind of work. He did. Over the next months, we reworked the manuscript until I felt it had a real chance to be published. I showed it to my editor again, and she wanted to meet with me and Ross and discuss ideas for more revisions. Finally, after over a year of corresponding by email, Ross and I would meet for the first time. Great.

Ross looked the way he described himself in the novel. Here was a thoughtful, well-mannered young man who had coauthored a book and who was taking notes as *our* editor spoke. She had a laundry list of changes she wanted. We made them over the next months. No big deal for me—it's what I do—and Ross continued to stay with it.

This is what I learned from Ross: Some writers, even if they are young, can handle working on a longer piece of writing such as a novel. Their writing will probably reflect their actual lives. A young writer will have more trouble writing outside his or her experience. Most of all, I learned that the writing process, properly managed, can be successfully navigated, given the necessary time commitment and interest. Our book, *Kick*, was published in 2011.

I think few young people could juggle a school schedule, play on a sports team, and write a novel in their spare time, as Ross did. During his junior year of high school, we were still doing last-minute revisions. It takes work, and dedication, and more work. But it's possible. It's a life to which I've grown accustomed, one Ross has accepted, and one I hope you'll challenge yourself to accept as well.

Welcome to the profession!

CHAPTER 2

SOMETHING OLD, SOMETHING NEW,
SOMETHING BORROWED, SOMETHING BLUE

I'd like to talk more with you about "decoding" and "ownership." I mentioned that I don't feel that the decoding process ends with simply understanding the dictionary definition of a word or the rules of English grammar. In many ways, I feel like my life has been a continual quest to get better and better at decoding by learning more about the world around me. For me, this means getting to know the young people I write about and who read my books.

I remember my own teen years, of course, but that's not enough. It's a different world today, and to make sure my readers can decode my books, I know I need to understand where they're coming from, too. It starts with who I am and my point of view. Everything I've ever done in my life eventually affects the way I write, and what my work with young people has taught me over the years is what I write about. We've already talked about me living in Harlem with the Dean family. My childhood was happy, and I didn't make much of the racial composition of either my family or my neighborhood. I went to school with all kinds of kids, and I mostly enjoyed the experience. My best friend was German American, and his family owned a bakery a few blocks from me. His mom was especially generous with the chocolate chip cookies I liked. But there were other things going on in my head that I didn't realize at the time. It took me years to figure these things out.

Reading and writing changed my life, and as a writer I try to connect with young people through my own books. I hope that I've been able to reach some of you. Writing about characters based on my own experiences has taught me more about that time in my life. I know myself more deeply because of you, my readers.

I have been lucky enough to be successful at what I love to do, which has enabled me to spend most of my time doing it. My success at writing is due to my intelligence and my willingness to work hard, and the values and wisdom I've been handed from previous generations.

My work ethic and sense of responsibility were ingrained by my father, my love of stories was fostered by my mother, and my belief in my writing abilities was reinforced by my teacher. The library branch where I spent countless hours of my childhood reading was built long before I was born. I don't take these experiences for granted, and I hope that by mentoring teenagers, I can show my gratitude to the people who changed the course of my life.

In school I learned American history (which I loved), and I read as much as I could. What I was doing, though, was reading about other cultures, about people whose race was different from mine. There were no books about Harlem in my school, and no books about black people. Without really thinking about it much, I made the decision that black people just weren't that important. I did understand that education was important and noticed that the few black people who were doing well had all gone to college. So I decided that, since I was pretty smart, I would go to college, too. One day.

Until then I would just be me. I loved playing basketball, and you could find me at the playground or in the school gym as much as possible. I even thought of playing professional basketball one day. Or, if I couldn't play professional basketball, perhaps I could play pro baseball. I was a sports guy. The sports books I read weren't written on the same level as my other books, but they were exciting and I could imagine myself in them.

My home life revolved around the family. My dad was a hardworking man who had a job with the same company for years. My mom did a variety of jobs and liked to read true romance stories. My big sisters read comics and practiced their dancing in our tidy little living room in the afternoons. My dad insisted that the family have dinner together every evening, and I enjoyed that, too. Here is where I would hear about what the rest of the family had experienced during the day and their comments. I didn't know at the time that these dinnertime chats would influence my life.

The neighborhood was also part of my life. I saw what people were doing and how they lived. Somewhere deep inside, I made judgments, too. I thought there were "smart" people and "ordinary" people. I didn't know anything about IQ and I didn't think anybody was particularly dumb. And along with my judgments of others, I began to judge myself. Yes, I thought I was a "smart" person. Not bad looking, either. And one of the things I knew that "smart" people did was read, so I was proud of that part of my life. What I find interesting today is how much I didn't know (then).

I have found that people can sometimes be limited both in their experiences and in their outlook. You may never have had the opportunity to venture out of your own neighborhood, state, or country. While interviewing young people in correctional institutions, I was surprised to discover that many had never been outside their communities until they were transported to an out-of-city facility after being convicted of a crime. Few of them had been exposed to the around-the-dinner-table talks that were part of my growing-up experience. So much of what I had thought about came from these talks. Even if I didn't agree with my parents' point of view, I knew what their opinions would be. I didn't have to experience every situation to have a fair idea of what to do if I faced it. I believe that many of these young people would not have been involved in crime if they had had a wider experience.

A book can provide opportunities to discuss issues without the reader actually living through the events in the book. This is how I was mentored growing up. Although my parents had direct conversations with me concerning how they expected me to act, far more time was spent commenting on the behavior of others. When a teenage girl in the neighborhood became pregnant, my father's remarks on how difficult life would be for both the girl and the baby gave me a different perspective on the situation.

A young boy, a friend of mine, was caught up in drugs. My father pointed out the hurt and pain he was causing himself and his family. Another friend bragged about the money he was making after dropping out of school. My father asked me what I thought would happen if there was a great job available and the employer wanted a high school graduate. These conversations were how I learned family values.

As a rebellious teenager, I didn't listen to all of my family's advice. I had my own issues, such as a speech defect, a quick temper, and a financial situation that meant that I would not be able to go to college. I often did the wrong thing, but I grew up knowing the right things. With maturity, the values that I "knew" became the values that I lived.

Too many young people don't grow up in stable family situations, let alone have a dinner table around which the family gathers. Television stories can sometimes substitute for these talks, as can newspaper articles, but books, for a number of reasons, are ideal for this purpose.

In each of my novels, my main character confronts a problem. I try to explore that character's feelings as well as the problem. I want to create characters who readers will feel they know and understand. The mind and feelings of a well-drawn character become the common ground between the author and the readers.

From talking to thousands of young people and reading letters from teenagers all over the world, I have seen how young people identify with characters in books. This places an awesome responsibility on the author but also provides an amazing opportunity to reach out and connect with someone else.

Many young people caught up in the judicial system had simply drifted into a dangerous encounter that they didn't know how to handle. Others had given in to peer pressure by joining a shady adventure. Some had just allowed themselves to act too quickly in a risky situation. But few had had the luxury of talking about these situations beforehand and considering the possible consequences. They hadn't had the conversations that would have warned them to be cautious. When I saw these scenarios over and over again, I knew I wanted to write about them.

In my visits to courtrooms and juvenile and adult jails, I've noted that many of the defendants and inmates are not aware of the seriousness of their crimes. They think their guilt depends on their intent and not on the ultimate result of their activity. At one trial I attended, a young man was "carrying" his father's gun for the day. An older boy took it from him and said he was going to rob a newsstand. The younger boy, thinking he'd be able to put the gun back before his father got home, went with the older boy to the robbery and helped distract the clerk while the other boy slipped behind the counter. The older boy shot and killed the clerk. While the younger boy did not intend for the clerk to be killed (or even robbed), he was charged with murder. Was this fair? It doesn't matter, because the law establishes responsibility for all participants. I found this fascinating and a bit disturbing, something I wanted to think about and write about.

In my book *Monster*, I wrote about a young man who doesn't want to be considered unmanly and, when given an opportunity to participate in a caper in what he sees as a minor role, does so. He is asked to go into a grocery store, see if any police are present, and walk out. He is not asked to do anything else. When the "get over" goes wrong and the grocer is killed, the young hero is surprised to find himself on trial as an accomplice to murder.

The book gave me the chance to write something about peer pressure, decision making, morality, and the legal/judicial system. I simply took the problem I saw in real life and gave it to Steve Harmon.

Writers stretch the imaginations of their readers to take in unfamiliar scenarios and environments. As a young reader, I found the books of Anatole France and Ernest Hemingway fascinating. I loved *The Red Badge of Courage* by Stephen Crane and enjoyed the vicarious experience of running with him through the woods during the Civil War. But I also learned things from these books—about how other people felt and how they experienced their humanity—that I could use throughout my own life.

I want to begin each of my novels with an interesting character who has an interesting problem. Not all of my characters will be interesting to everyone, and they don't need to be. You should be interested in the character and the problem. They both should be important to you. If the character is interesting enough, then your readers will be interested in him/her/it. If the character is interesting enough and the problem is interesting enough, you might even get the book published.

So what I am doing, like what every writer does, I suspect, is bringing pieces of my own life and my own viewpoints to the page. Writers might borrow from their own pasts or the pasts of friends or relatives, and even from other writers. I loved Walt Whitman's poetry so much that I used some of his techniques when I wrote *We Are America*.

I hope to bring something new to each book by how I approach the problem, or how I approach the writing. In *Monster* I use a screen-writing technique. This came from a series of interviews I did in a maximum-security prison in which the inmates spoke of their personal lives in the first person and of the crimes they had committed in the third person. Steve, in *Monster*, speaks of himself and how he feels in the first person but quickly switches to the screen format when he talks about the crime.

I always encourage writers to bring as much of themselves to their writing as possible. You are what makes the book interesting, your particular point of view. In *Kick* the character created by Ross was fascinating to me, and I looked forward to reading each of his chapters. The character is not like Ross, but Ross's ideas and personality formed the character into one of the most interesting I've read about.

For me, reading James Baldwin's story "Sonny's Blues" gave me permission to write about my Harlem neighborhood and allowed me to explore that part of my life. I didn't know I needed that permission until I read Baldwin's story.

A confession. Although my method of writing seems fairly straightforward and somewhat methodical, there is also another factor: daydreaming. I spend a lot of time daydreaming, and I enjoy it almost as much as I enjoy writing. My head is usually full of me playing ball if I'm working on a sports book, or storming a beach if I am writing a war novel, or solving a mystery if that is what I'm writing about. The outlines help me to control the daydreams, and they also help me to finish the important first draft.

To sum up what I want/need from a first draft: first, an interesting character. This could be a person, an animal, or even a place. In *The Old Man and the Sea*, Hemingway uses the sea as a character. Then we need an interesting problem. We can't assume that the reader will continue turning pages—we have to provide the reason. Finally, we need the journey and, hopefully, some growth along the way. The journey is simply what it seems to be, a trip from where the character begins to where he or she ends up. It's the quality of this journey that makes the story publishable.

Having your writing published is one of the most exciting parts of being a writer. It's fun knowing that there are people who actually want to read what you have written, and even more fun knowing that many will enjoy your writing. You will get feedback, some of it positive and some not, but most of it will at least be somewhat interesting. If your school has a literary magazine or a newspaper, that can be a great way to start getting your writing published. If your school doesn't have a literary magazine, maybe you could start one. Writing for publication will help you hone your writing skills. You'll become accustomed to keeping your audience in mind while writing, and be forced to think about how to engage your readers.

When I met thirteen-year-old Ross Workman through email correspondence, I noticed several interesting things about him. Through his physical activities (he was a serious soccer player and wrestler), he had more of what I call life *range* than many young people his age. And in his emails about my work, he demonstrated an understanding of structure and what I was trying to do with that structure.

My initial invitation to Ross to work together was like my own early writing efforts—I had no high expectations, but I did think it would be an enjoyable experience for both of us. I knew I was right when Ross quickly grasped the structure I suggested and kept that structure firmly in mind as we proceeded. We wrote alternating chapters, and I saw that he was bringing himself to the project with a great deal of enthusiasm. Up to a point.

We had reached a not-too-difficult chapter in the second draft of the novel. When I challenged what seemed to be a hastily written revision, he expressed discouragement. We were halfway through the second set of revisions (there would be another draft) and he was in the unfamiliar position of rereading his first chapters and sensing that they were weak. He was asking himself if he was a real writer and questioning his ability to improve.

It was unfamiliar territory to Ross, but not to me. I knew that when Ross and I had lived with the characters in *Kick* through a couple of drafts, our first impressions of them would have deepened, and that the situations we put them in would have slightly different meanings to us as we moved along. Ross was experiencing the natural progression of a writer. Most of my revisions are in the first part of a manuscript. If it takes me months to complete a draft, then it has also given me those months of knowing the characters and their lives.

Now a sixteen-year-old who had grown both physically and emotionally, Ross would of course see his characters differently, because he was a different person.

I came away from the experience of writing *Kick* with Ross somewhat amazed that he could sustain his part in this novel and still keep up a demanding school program, athletics, and family life. I also saw his growth process as something I should consider in everything I write. Am I the same person finishing the book as I was starting it? Should I plan to revisit the first chapters of every book? Interesting.

I believe that Ross's next book will be better because of his work with me. I believe my next book will be better because of my work with Ross.

CHAPTER 3

HELLO, VOICES IN MY HEAD

As a writer, I live in an imagined world. There characters wander in and out of story contexts to expose some idea, some random flight of fancy that holds some fascination for me, at least for the duration of the writing project. But I also live in a physical world. Eating, spending time on the line at my bank— these are mere interruptions that I suffer until I can get back to the real world inside my head.

You never know exactly where your next idea will come from. I personally spend a minimum of five hours per day dreaming of cool stuff I'd like to be doing. I keep a notebook by my bed and pens (at least two) along the bed rails so when an idea comes in the middle of the night, I don't even have to get up to record it.

My summers in Harlem were mainly focused on street games. We played basketball in the playground across the street, stickball between the sewers around the corner, and handball against the church wall. When it rained or when it was too hot for other kids to play ball (it was never too hot for me!), I would make the trek to the George Bruce Branch of the New York Public Library. All writers find their foundation in reading, and I've always found time for books. At some point in my life, I decided to read all the books in the library. I quickly realized that this was a mountain of books to tackle. But once a week, I would try to get to the library and carefully select the four books I was allowed to take out at a time.

Books filled my time nicely. They amused me. Some books I even found delightful. Though I was unaware of it at the time, they were also telling me some interesting things about myself. To begin with, I was not nearly as unique a person as I had thought. There were other people who wondered whether they were attractive or not, and others who felt alone in the world. Some of the books told me that there were people who lived in foreign lands who sometimes despaired of their lives and their chances for success. Other books told me of people who had lived long before me who worried about the same problems that I had felt could only be mine. By the time I was fifteen, I was beginning to realize that the singular viewpoint of my life was only a small part of a much larger world.

I was also learning other mundane things. A biography of a Chinese philosopher-poet told me how he struggled to achieve but also how he traveled through China and how the government worked there. A novel translated from French told me how difficult life was in Paris in 1819 and led me to finding that city on the map.

In years to come, I would also discover that the secondary things I had found in books would be part of my casual conversation with other people who read and that the books experienced by others would be the basis of new friendships.

My summer reading added greatly to the person I was during that time. I was not only a ball-playing athlete, but I had developed an entirely new dimension. As important as sports were to me, and they remained that important for years, the new perspectives provided by the books I read eventually became even more vital to my life. I have never climbed that entire mountain of books, but I have used many books to enrich and expand all the seasons of my life.

The second main source of inspiration for me is through meeting young people like you and listening to your stories. When I listen to your concerns, it helps me understand what you need from me as an author. It gives me ideas about what kinds of characters interest you and which stories you'll be able to relate to.

On a visit to a juvenile detention facility in the South Bronx a few years ago, I met a young girl named Brittany. She told me she had found a sense of "family" in prison. She said that being locked up allowed her to think more, and to think more positively. With the opportunity for reflection came self-realization. I asked Brittany to outline a book and send it to me so I could help her with it. When I asked her what I should write about in my next book, she told me I was doing it already, that I should write about "life, just life."

When I was writing *Lockdown*, a novel about a teen in juvenile detention, I thought a lot about Brittany and the many kids like her I had met over the years. I knew they were going to be the ones reading my book, and I wanted to make sure I was being true to their stories. The more I know about young people in juvenile facilities, the more I want to see if I can make some kind of difference in their lives.

The best way to find inspiration is just to live your life doing those things that interest you most. Figure out what you like to do, and go out and do it. If you like a certain sport, kind of music, or volunteer activity, explore it and think about what it does for you and about how to share your experience through writing. Pursuing your passions will expand your world. This will make you a better writer. You can find inspiration everywhere. The trick is to keep your eyes open.

CHAPTER 4

MAP IT OUT

There are two methods of finishing a book. The first is to make a plan in your head. This works for some people. For me, it's helpful to make a plan on paper.

After twenty years of writing at night, I began seriously considering the idea of becoming a full-time writer when I was laid off from my job at a publishing house. My wife encouraged me to use the opportunity to freelance. I figured out pretty quickly that if I wanted to make money as a writer, I would need to develop a structured schedule for myself.

Here's how I do it:

First, I submit my book idea to a publisher. If the editor thinks the idea is good, I spend about a month shaping the book in my mind. This sounds like a lot of daydreaming, but in fact is a lot of hard work.

For you as a writer, you'll just have to trust that your idea is interesting. If it interests you, that's probably a good sign that you're on the right track. You could talk about your idea to someone whose opinion you value. Pay attention to the questions they ask you and try to work out the kinks. Or you could dream up a character in your head who is your book editor. Discuss your ideas with this imaginary editor and challenge yourself with the questions you imagine an editor might ask you.

On the facing notebook page, I listed some of the ideas I was thinking about and imagined what my editor might think of them. I have a living, breathing editor, so I knew that eventually I would share my ideas. In the privacy of my own notebook, though, I simply imagined what my editor might think. You can do the same.

The next step is to think a little more deeply about your idea. I do this by changing my idea into a problem that the main character is going to face. Creating a problem forces me to examine whether my initial idea

Editing Process —
Do you tell your editor what you're
trying to do?

2. 2 Beast
1. 3/2 Legend of Tarik
3. Game

Legend

AN African Hero based on a real African
Phlicia Rashad =
Springboard — Crude
Editor — Heard = Fantasy

Beast

Inner City — coming to the realization of
what it means to a black male in America
w/o education and his need to address
his strategies and responsibilities

Heard — Drugs?

Game

Relationship Between Drew & his father —
It is an essentially loving relationship
but with an aura of disappointment
Mother + Loving
Sister — Loving but and allies
Ruffy — Loving
Tony — Tony represents — his ghosts of
Christmas future

is complex enough and interesting enough.

The facing page is from one of the notebooks I kept when I was writing *Game*, a novel about a basketball player who is having problems with his coach and is losing his best-player status to the new Czech kid on the team.

You can see that I start by trying to turn my idea into a problem for the main character. I started with a vague idea and tried to hone it into the question: "Suppose someone you're connected with—a teacher, a coach, a classmate—simply doesn't like you that much?" This was really early prewriting, and I wasn't even sure it would end up being a book. I tried to challenge the writer in me by asking myself, "Is this a novel?"

The notes also show that while I'm thinking about the problem, I'm simultaneously shaping the book's main character. I don't just do this in my head. I look for photographs to find physical representations of my characters. I cut these out, and my wife creates a collage of them, which I hang on the wall over my computer. I like to use oaktag. Looking at my characters while I'm doing my thinking makes me feel like they've moved in and we're really getting to know one another. They become real people to me, freeing up my imagination to flesh out their personalities and lives.

Writing - The Y.A. Novel

Begins w/ Problem

Suppose someone you're connected with - a teacher, a coach, a classmate, simply doesn't like you that much?

Suppose your life isn't going the way you want it to go? Actually, suppose it sucked?

Drew's life should be going well, but instead it sucks.

Drew has dual cognitions

Life is good	Neighborhood is poor
You can be anything you choose to be	His neighbors, especially men, are bad off
Life is fair	Life doesn't seem fair
All people are created equal	White people have it good
The Best people succeed	His skills are negated by someone else's choices

Is this a Novel?
   Six Box Outline
   30 Box Outline - Carrier problem

Who is my character?
   Define my character by discussing his surroundings - He has a family -
        Family
        He has friends
             Friends

Once I feel I have solid characters, I'll expand the problem into a rough outline consisting of six boxes.

SIX-BOX MODEL FOR FICTION

1. **CHARACTER** **& PROBLEM**	**2** **OBVIOUS** **SOLUTIONS**	**3** **INSIGHT &** **INNER CONFLICT**
4 **GROWTH &** **CHANGE**	**5** **TAKING ACTION**	**6** **RESOLUTION**

Box 1: Introduce the main character and the problem he faces.

Box 2: Explain why the problem is complex and can't be solved by any simple solutions.

Box 3: Explain why it's so important that the main character figure out a solution to the problem.

Box 4: Show the main character undergoing change of some sort.

Box 5: Show the main character deciding to do something about the problem and taking action.

Box 6: Show how everything turns out for the main character.

In the next few chapters, I'll show you how I outline and flesh out each box so you'll be able to use this method with your own story ideas.

WENDY

Walking on the Front Door

Boy wants to go to College	Studies Hard Cheat Scheme	Gets smart girlfriend
What is smart? Smart is what People Do	Sets out to convince Dean he is smart enough w/ caper	Gets into College

Sometimes I have a lot of trouble filling in the six boxes. I take this as a clue that my problem might not be interesting enough, and I'll go back and try to make it more complicated. I know I've thought of a problem that is complicated enough when the way the main character works out the solution paves the way for the plot of the rest of the book and leads me to the ending.

Thinking deeply about the problem will force you to think about the entire story. If you make the character and the problem interesting enough, your reader will want to read on to see how it all comes out. If the problem is clear and the motivation comes from the character's inner self, you're halfway home. Don't worry about it if you have an idea that you end up not liking. Just throw it out and start over. You can make changes and rewrites as you go along.

CHAPTER 5

LIGHTS, CAMERA, ACTION!

If I'm happy with my rough outline—it usually takes a few tries to get it to this point—I'll expand it by breaking each of the six boxes up into scenes. For a short story, I shoot for between three and six scenes, no more than one scene per box. For a novel, it will be more like thirty or forty, which means I usually start with about five scenes per box.

The way I do it is sort of like laying out a movie. What this scene-by-scene breakdown does for me is twofold. First, it forces me to keep thinking through my story more and more deeply.

Second, it gives me a chance to put some action

into my plot. It doesn't have to be martial arts, but a story is always better if something is going on. For me, it's one of the most exciting parts of planning the book, because I get to imagine the events of the story in detail, not just in theory. I've always written books with a lot of action in them. I think action makes the book better and keeps the reader hooked. It also makes the book more fun to write.

On the following pages you'll see an example of a scene-by-scene outline I did for *All the Right Stuff*, a novel about how Paul picks up the street version of political philosophy while working at a soup kitchen.

For each scene, I think first about what piece of the story I want to include. This gives me a goal for the scene. Is this the first scene in the book? Then my goal might be to show something specific I want the reader to know about my character. Is it the first time the reader is finding out about the problem? I'll want to make sure the reader is engaged right away.

Next I think about who is going to be in the scene. Which characters need to appear to move the story forward? If it's the first time the reader is meeting the main character's parents, for example, what do I need to show the reader about them?

Once I know which characters I want to bring into

From 88 —

1. Jimmy Begins the Oyster Gumbo
   One page —
   He is nervous —
   How much ~~to put on~~ chicken, ham,
   + Oysters to put in?
   Elijah — these people know the difference
   between soup + stew. Your job here
   is to make soup.

2. Elijah — The people benefit from the
   soup in a way that I have
   decided is good. They share that
   experience to a degree because they
   keep returning. They come here for:
         1. Companionship
         2. The Soup — Because it's good
         3. The Diversion
         4. The meal

3. a. Some people would prefer stew to
   soup and they've expressed ~~that~~
   to me. I still do soup.
   b. Different time
   c. Different soups

4. Some community people think that
   everybody should be included +
   get mad about it.

5. Some people get mad at me
   because I'm not doing enough for
   the community.

6. I've been robbed twice.
         1. Accused of getting government money
         2. Rich

7. What would happen if everybody had an equal voice?
   a - I probably couldn't continue
   b - People would be angry w/me.
   c - loss of benefits
   D - No contract is possible

8. People who come here have to give up the rights to decide what soup they get, when, etc.

9. Is it fair?
   a - Everybody is treated equally
   b. They don't necessarily get what they want
   c. They do benefit.
   d. The contract continues according to my rules
   e. We live in peace.

Jimmy serves his Jumbo -

Woman says that Jumbo saved a man's life. They were gonna hang him His Mama didn't know what to do she was so upset. She made him some soup & he felt so good he came out of his despair & the old white devil that he had lynched drums, said he would forgive him for a dollar. "We scrambled around and got up that dollar & the boy came home -

People leave. They wash dishes —
Serving feeling good.

1. Sly — The Will to Eminence
The Soupare society makes is
the same as my songs. I choose to
make it soup, and our society makes
rules that benefit most people
most of the time.
What it says that all people
are equal if they do things in the
manner we say. If anybody came
in here today looking for corned
beef and cabbage they were disappointed.
But if they came in looking for just
a good bowl of soup they were
pleased.
Sly looked around and said that
he didn't want to follow the road
that led to equal because he could
do better on another road. In
other words he didn't give up his
privilege of choosing. And his
right — the society does make a
theme of things they don't like.

the scene, that helps me figure out the setting. If I need to introduce the main character's best friend to the reader, it might be logical for the scene to take place at school or right after school. This is where it really becomes like a movie. Try to picture the surroundings of the characters in the scene in as much detail as possible. Sometimes it helps me to look at photographs while I'm creating scenes in my mind. The same way photographs help me keep my characters consistent, they also help me with consistency in the action. Photographs can also give you ideas. Are the characters in a park? Which park? What are they looking at? Are they sitting or standing? What's going on around them?

After I set the scene, I think about what exactly will happen and how it will go down. In life, people are almost always doing at least two things at once. Writers need to remember to add action to a scene. When I was writing *Kick* with Ross, I was having trouble with one chapter in particular (chapter nine). I knew that I wanted the scene to include the main character and his mentor. My goal was to show the reader that this was the first time the main character began opening up and trusting his mentor. I wrote the scene a few times, but it was very heavy on dialogue and it didn't have the sense of urgency I wanted. I decided to have the main character take a physical fitness test during the scene. That did the trick. With this action in place, I could pace the dialogue so that the characters were speaking in quick bursts of conversation between drills. It made the dialogue more rushed and chaotic. As the main character became more and more physically exhausted, his emotional defenses broke down.

As I'm shopping, or listening to my favorite radio station, I'm keeping my mind open to ways to make my scene breakdown richer. Instead of having two ninth graders talking in the media center, perhaps I could have them talking while playing chess or tennis. That way I have an additional action, which I might be able to incorporate into the scene and add interest or even set up a new scene.

Writing about sports is one of my favorite ways to incorporate action into a scene. I happen to love to write about sports. Basketball was a huge part of my youth, and I still attend high school basketball games and tournaments. I go to high school games because I like high school basketball and I like watching the kids involve themselves in the game as spectators. Some of the plays that appear in my books are ones I made up, some are from my own playing days, which are now past, and some are from coaching tapes. If there's something in particular you like to do, you can bring that action into your book. Write about what you know.

If I've been able to expand my outline scene by scene, I know I have a really good idea that has the potential to be an entire book. What I've done is create a map for myself so that I will be able to get from the beginning of the book to the end. I don't want to just start writing and lose my way somewhere in the middle.

With my map in hand, I embark on the task of stringing words and sentences together and getting the story down in the form of a first draft. I've been doing this for a long time, so my first draft is usually pretty close to the final version. When I started out, though, this wasn't always the case. Revision is the most important part of the process.

Early in my career, I made a goal for myself of writing ten pages per day. Usually, I meet this goal. In recent years, I have cut my goal to five pages per day. This gives me more time to daydream and to annoy my family.

You might feel you're overthinking things at this point. I always overthink *everything*. Having an imaginative thrust is what I believe led me to being a writer. Don't get lost, but also don't be afraid of over-thinking. Let your mind wander and your imagination run around.

One last piece of advice before you take the plunge: Don't be hesitant. You're trying to produce a written piece where there was only a blank page before. Don't worry about mistakes. You have to be willing to make mistakes. I'll try anything to see if it works. If it does, I'm really pleased. If it doesn't, I blame it on my cat (she gets a percentage of my royalties!). Or fate. Or whatever. The important thing is to keep moving on to the next step. Go for it!

CHAPTER 6

Nice to Meet You

I have a few tried-and-true techniques I use to create my characters. You already know that characters are supposed to be "three-dimensional." This means that each character must seem like a real, live person with all the many facets of an inner life that you'd recognize in, say, your best friend. Once you start actually writing, you'll face the challenge of making a reader see your characters as three-dimensional. Long before you're ready to introduce your characters to readers, you need to get to know them yourself.

My method is to find photos of my characters and make a collage. The photos help me make up further details about my characters and help me to stay consistent.

One of my hobbies is collecting antique photographs. When I was teaching a writing class many years ago, I asked my students to bring in photos of their grandparents as children. The kids loved the photographs. They wanted to learn why their grandparents would wear those kinds of clothes and shoes, and what types of houses they lived in. The kids were so responsive that I remember thinking, There's something special about photos. I need to use photos as part of my writing technique.

After I have my collage, I create word portraits of each character. I write a paragraph or so per character, but sometimes my hero gets a longer portrait. Try to make this portrait as detailed as possible. Pretend you're really meeting this person for the first time, and think of the kinds of questions you'd ask. Actually, meeting your characters is better than meeting real people, because you don't have to worry about being polite. You can ask anything you want—the more personal, the better.

Through your word portraits, you'll answer these questions. It works well for me to start with the big stuff, like where the character lives, how old he is, where he was born, what his parents are like. Then I'll move on to deeper questions, like how he feels and what he loves and hates and fears.

For example, when I wrote *Kick*, I thought about the character of Sergeant Brown having a wife and a dog and living in a largely suburban area. Maybe you want to create a character who is close to your own age. Come up with a bunch of questions you might want to ask about someone you just met in real life and transfer the answers to your character. What nationality is your character? What does he or she look like? How old is he or she? What's a typical day like for him or her? Where does he or she live? Who does he or she live with? What is he or she into? What's going well in his or her life, and what's going not so well? How does this affect him or her? Is he or she happy or sad? What are his or her hopes and dreams?

Then try to answer the questions you've posed. Keep asking more questions and coming up with more answers. The more complex you make your main character, the more interesting the book will be. Also, keep in mind that these are only ideas. All of the answers to your questions can change if you need them to change. Later.

The last thing I do is to make a time line for my

characters' lives. I start with what year I want the book to take place in and subtract the character's age to find out what year he was born. From there, I'll write a paragraph or so for each year of his life. This helps chronicle the main events of the character's life and gives a better sense of his or her personal history. You may get ideas for your story while you're doing the time line, because you'll see ways in which your character's history might affect his life and where he's coming from when the story starts. As you write, you may find better ideas. No problem. This process should be flexible, and fun.

On the next page is one of my time lines. I laid this out when I was writing *All the Right Stuff*. It shows the life of the main character's father, Richard DuPree.

For teen writers, I've found out that it may be easier to try to write about a main character who is similar to you in personality, interests, even appearance. Since you understand exactly how the character feels, you can write about him or her more realistically. Kevin, the hero of *Kick*, plays soccer, just like the teen coauthor, Ross Workman. We thought Kevin, who is half Irish and half Colombian, would look completely Colombian. But Ross wasn't sure how a character who looked completely Colombian would feel. Ross himself

Father - Richard Dupree

DOB - Aug 1972

14	Aug 1986 - Spofford Possession
18	Aug 1990 - Rikers Distribution
24	Aug 1996 - Impregnates wife
25	May 1997 - Jimmy Born
27	Aug 1999 - Lives w/Jimmy
29	Aug 2001 Rikers Aggravated Assault
31	Aug 2003 Greenhaven
37	Aug 2009 Release Armed Robbery
39	Mar 2012 Killed

is part Colombian, but he has brown hair, blue eyes, and light skin. We decided to make the character half Colombian but fair-skinned, like Ross.

You already know that I didn't always get along well with other kids when I was in school. I love making up characters in my head and getting to know them. What you're really doing is developing your own decoding and ownership skills in yet another way. If you can dream up a person and give him or her a real personality and identity, congratulations—you have a rich imagination and a great deal of human empathy. Because they are products of your own mind, the closer you become to your characters, the more you're learning about yourself. Nice work.

CHAPTER 7

WHAT'S GOING ON?

This is the first box in your outline, and will be the first section of your story.

You have two main goals for what you want to establish: a character or characters so interesting that the reader will want to know more about them, and a problem serious enough that the reader will share the character's concern. You want to give the reader a reason to continue reading.

Concentrate on a problem that will interest the reader. What has happened? Why did your character behave the way he did? Who are the other characters and how are they involved? Once you've thought about the problem and expanded this section into five or six scenes, you're ready to start writing.

Action will be your best friend throughout the book, but especially in this first section. There is so much to get down. Think analytically about how you want to do this. Have you ever heard someone describe a story as "unfolding"? This is your goal as a writer. You want your story to happen on the page. This starts in your head. It really helps me if I'm relaxed. Some writers say they prefer to be slightly physically tired before starting to write. I personally like to write in the early morning, after a brisk walk. Maybe you like to write late at night, or exactly at noon every day. Take a deep breath. Stare off into space for a little while and then come back to your computer screen, notebook— wherever you put down your words.

Sometimes when I'm writing the first section of a book, I'll start to get ahead of myself. I've just done so much great thinking about everything that's going to happen later on in the book, and I'll start to shove too much information into the first section. Try to slow it down. The reader should emerge from this section with a lot of questions about what is happening with the main character and with a lot of empathy for him or her. If you have a truly interesting character and a compelling problem, the writing process remains interesting to you, too.

For now, one of the most important things you can keep in mind is that your readers know something about your character, and they understand the problem but don't see where the solution lies. Reading your book or story will be their reward for being curious. You've already done all this thinking and daydreaming about your book, so a lot of the piece you're working on is in your head already. Try not to make assumptions about what your reader knows. For example, when I wrote *Game*, which is about a basketball team, I assumed that my readers knew nothing about the sport I was writing about. Many of my readers are sports fans, but if I have done my job as a writer correctly, someone who doesn't follow sports should also be able to follow the story and enjoy reading it, too.

Also keep in mind the flow of your story. Sometimes, when you're introducing new characters or describing a scene, it can be challenging to make your writing sound natural. I often try to come up with a detail about a character before I actually bring him or her on the scene.

CHAPTER 8

WHERE'S THE FIRE?

There are usually obvious ways to solve a problem, but a story wouldn't be very interesting if the problem had a simple solution. Try to make the problem as complex as possible. You introduced the problem in Box 1, and now in Box 2 you're going to expand on it and show the reader why it's so complicated.

Think about what kinds of questions you would ask if someone was telling you about the problem. For example, maybe you have a friend who wants to go to a concert but doesn't have the money for the ticket. A lot of simple solutions might come to mind. Can he borrow the money from someone and pay that person back? Is he too proud to ask anyone to lend him money? How come? Is there any way for him to make some money in time for the concert? Why not?

Choose a problem with depth so that readers will be more invested in finding out how the main character figures out a solution.

The most compelling complexities will have to do with the main character's own limitations and motivations. Show the reader why this character and his particular situation are unique. You're letting the reader learn more about the problem and more about the main character while raising the stakes.

In Box 2 the main character probably won't have a lot of insight. I keep in mind examples I have seen in my own life. After dropping out of high school at seventeen and knocking around for years in various jobs, I decided, at the age of about forty, to go to SUNY Empire State College.

I was going to major in communications, but with whom was I going to communicate? I was interested in people from my own background—poorer people— and a teacher suggested that I do interviews with street people. I did some, but then I decided to go to prisons. I recorded six hundred pages of interviews with prisoners in New York and New Jersey. And patterns began to emerge. The inmates knew why they were in jail—they knew what crimes they had committed or had been accused of committing—but they never seemed to be really sure of the path that had led them there.

You don't wake up one morning and say, "I've got a good idea. Today I'll think I'll commit armed robbery." There's a slippery slope. You do the small crimes, and then you sort of give yourself permission to go on. I talked to defense attorneys and prosecutors, and they all said the same thing: that no one starts off as a murderer. They all start with small crimes and work their way up.

The prisoners felt that they were good people. They were always talking about whether they were guilty or innocent. They could discuss the nuances of their cases as if they were jailhouse lawyers, so to speak, and they knew the law backward and forward. But there was never any talk about moral context.

One day, I was watching a trial in Jersey City in which a seventeen-year-old boy was charged with armed robbery and attempted murder. The courthouse is right across from a high school, and I could hear the kids getting out of class. And then it hit me: Here's this frightened young boy on trial, and it's incredible how some kids could go from being in high school to facing a life sentence not much later.

I saw that the prisoners I interviewed were separating their actions, their crimes, from who they were as people. One interesting guy was a soldier who had four years of college. He and some others forced their way into a house, and there was a fight. He told the judge at sentencing (and this is a fairly common comment), "Well, I wouldn't have shot him, but he went for my gun." This guy was separating the idea of his having killed someone from who he was as a person. So he was saying, "I wouldn't have killed him; it was his fault that he was killed."

The main character in Box 2 will be like these prisoners. He won't fully understand how to solve his problem and probably won't fully understand the problem itself.

CHAPTER 9

WHAT'S IT TO YOU?

Once you have established that the simple solutions to the problem won't work for your character, you're ready for the third box. Your objective in Box 2 was to show how complicated the problem is. Your objective in Box 3 is to show how complicated the main character is.

In this section, you'll learn even more about the main character, and the reader will, too. You'll need to show why the character wants what he wants and make it clear why it's so vital that he solve his problem. Your character will take stock of who he is and how he has become the person he is now. He might think about his past and worry about his future.

But we're stuck in the limited universe of the book, so you have to make sure the plot is moving along as well. What is going on in the story, and how does your character feel about it? Think about what transitions your character needs to make to demonstrate the growth the reader is looking for. What is going on with the other characters in the book, such as the main character's family or friends? Is the main character feeling stronger or more capable of dealing with his problem? What is happening to him that is making him feel stronger? Does he have a different attitude? Why?

As your main character grows, learns, and explores his inner feelings, you and the reader will also grow, learn, and explore. Think about why you read a book. You want to connect with the character's situation and inner life and maybe learn something along the way. When you're writing, keep in mind that the reader will only keep reading as long as there's a payoff. The payoff is seeing the growth of the main character and seeing him change. Box 3 is about setting the stage for this to happen. The more you reveal about the main character in this section, the bigger the payoff will be in the next.

In Box 3 you might give your character another chance to try to solve the problem. Make sure his strategy is more complicated than the simple solutions we already explored in Box 2.

What you are doing is creating suspense. You and your reader will understand more about your character and maybe even be able to pinpoint some of the things the character is doing wrong in his life. Because your reader will be able to anticipate the ways in which the character might change in the course of the book, your reader will want to keep reading to find out what happens.

Even though you and the reader have gained insight into your character and his motivations, the character himself hasn't yet changed. He's still trying to work through his problem, but he doesn't succeed. If you have given him a complicated inner life, you'll know him very well by now. Your main character will be primed and ready for something to happen that will truly change his perspective and prepare him to do something about his problem.

It might seem contradictory that the character gains insight but doesn't change. I think of a letter I received a few years ago from a young prisoner who had read one of my books. He wrote that he wished he had read this book before committing his crime because he would have understood more, not about the crime, but about his motivation for doing it.

What he got from reading my book was what you're trying to give your reader in Box 3. I write because I'm trying to help young people figure out the emotional landscape that they're traveling through. I'm trying to work on this for my own benefit as well.

Here is an example of how to give the reader insight into your character. Lil J is the main character in *Dope Sick*. Lil J is a drug user who is in denial that he is on a downward spiral. He is given a chance to change one moment in his life. This forces him to go back and examine everything he's done that has led him to his current situation (which is not a good place).

In the book, a concerned teacher tries to get through to Lil J. But Lil J doesn't feel he can confide in his teacher. When I wrote this scene, I thought about how hard it was for me to confide in my teachers when I was in high school. The first time I dropped out of school, the counselors asked me what was wrong. And I couldn't say that my home life was disintegrating. I wasn't going to go there with some teacher. So in *Dope Sick*, I showed how Lil J couldn't focus on school and couldn't talk to his teachers about it. The reader learned more about his home life and saw that his mom was an alcoholic and what Lil J had to do to take care of her. That gave the reader insight into Lil J's character. Maybe Lil J was even starting to see those connections himself, but he didn't have them worked out in his head quite yet.

While you're outlining and writing this section, you'll get the chance to know your character better and better. You might learn more about yourself, too, as your ideas develop and deepen. The more you invest in thinking about and writing this section, the more invested your readers will be in your story. Your readers will be rooting for the main character. The point of Box 3 is to show that the main character has conflicts that are holding him back from solving his problem. I was once told to put a sign on my door reminding me not to forget my gym shorts. The teacher assumed that I was simply negligent in forgetting to bring them twice a week. The truth was that I couldn't afford to buy them, so I just told him that I had forgotten to put them into my bag. My shame at being that poor would show up in Box 3. During this part of the story, you want your reader to understand exactly why the main character, as he stands, must look further for an answer.

CHAPTER 10

GET IT TOGETHER

In Box 4 you are ready for your character to truly grow and change.

Change might come about through some outside event that forces the character to make a decision. Or maybe something happens that forces him to face his own ideas head-on and reexamine his behavior. Usually there is some sort of crisis that makes this change necessary.

You'll have to go deep into your main character's feelings. Maybe something happens that is an emotional experience. Does he gain trust in another character for the first time? Does something happen to him that gives him a new perspective he didn't have before? Does something happen that lets him understand another character's feelings in a way he wasn't able to earlier?

Another way to think of Box 4 is that this is where the character gets a second chance. I am very big on second chances. I had one.

When I was writing *Lockdown*, I thought of it as a book about redemption. The main character is a kid who has landed in juvenile detention for stealing prescription pads—arguably a relatively small crime. Once he's in juvie, though, he can't seem to stay out of trouble. His sense of morality is challenged and he becomes very confused, partially because in his environment morality is twisted.

I wrote the book based on my interviews with the many young men I've visited in juvenile detention centers. Very often I will see these young people and wonder, "What got you here? How did you get to this bad place?"

When kids get into trouble, it's not the last thing they did that gets them there. It's an attitude that they come up with that leads them slowly down this path. In order to escape, at some point, they have to change. It's not so much a matter of whether or not they are released, because if they are released but don't change their attitude, they may end up back in the system. It's only when they realize that they have to take responsibility, and admit where they went wrong, that they can start moving in a new direction.

This is how it can work with drug use. In *Dope Sick*, I wanted to explore a character, Lil J, who was also on a slippery slope. As it is for all the drug users I have known, the future is a dismal prospect that Lil J can only hope to avoid. For drug users, any hit might be bad, any transaction might lead to violence, any needle is potentially the carrier of a slow and painful death. And yet they go on using.

I've known guys who claimed that they just had "chippies," or light use of drugs. Others were heavier into hard drugs and didn't pretend otherwise. What I didn't understand was how the confirmed addicts kept going back to drugs once they had kicked. And they all kicked occasionally, by either being arrested, being hospitalized, or being lucky enough to get into a rehab center.

In writing *Dope Sick*, I recalled all the scenarios I had witnessed, including the constant denials of guys who I knew had robbed their own families for drug money. During the times when they were clean, when they had yet another chance to turn their lives around, few of them ever seemed to make it.

In both of these situations—juvenile crime and drug use—I try to show readers characters who have to come to grips with what I call the social contract. They have to come to grips with the idea that they have responsibility for their own lives, no matter what. No matter what happens to them.

I use my own life as an example. I am a high school dropout, but I am now a successful professional. Any person can take the path I took. I don't consider myself extraordinarily bright or extraordinarily gifted, but I've learned things. When I tell kids about my background, the reaction is very often "If you can do this, with your background, if you have gone through these things, then I can, too." Through our writings, we can send the same sorts of messages. Readers can see a character overcome a problem and realize that maybe they can do the same thing in their own lives.

CHAPTER 11

So What Are You Going
to Do About It?

In Box 5 your character finally takes action. He or she has gained insight and undergone some sort of growth. Armed with everything he or she now knows, he or she is going to be forced to face the problem directly. He or she has to undergo transformation.

I have had many discussions with kids in juvenile detention about my book *Monster*. When I ask them, "So what's the story with Steve?" they come up with interesting answers about his legal guilt, but eventually some kid says that whether Steve's legally guilty or innocent doesn't make any difference; he is guilty because he showed up that day. And to me, that's the essence of the book. Apart from legal machinations, does Steve accept his moral responsibility for what he's done, or is he just trying to avoid it?

By Box 5 everything has changed. Even the problem may have changed, in a way. It's not always black and white, and the main character might not solve the problem in a direct way. Maybe he thinks of it differently now. Maybe, because he's changed, the problem isn't such a big problem for him anymore, even though it may still exist.

It's also possible that the character's insight and change will help him find a solution to the problem. If you have been able to create a three-dimensional character with a rich inner life, and you have shown the reader why the problem is truly interesting, and you have developed the main character, this change will be believable to the reader. The solution to the problem should not come out of nowhere.

Whether you decide to have your main character solve the problem or not is fine. Either way, he or she has become a different person and learned something he or she didn't know about himself or herself before. Character growth rewards the reader.

Dope Sick and many other books I have written have ambiguous endings because life is like that. Life is not "Okay, you've solved all your problems, lickety-split." Life is not "Today is over, tomorrow's a new beginning." But there is the possibility of a new beginning. There is the possibility of new hope and change. And what I would like to have in all my books is just this possibility of change.

CHAPTER 12

THEN WHAT HAPPENED?

So in Box 6 the problem is resolved, not necessarily solved. We have the chance to tie up the loose ends.

We've already had a big moment for the main character. He's undergone change, and he's faced his problem. We know that no matter what happens to him after this point, he's figured out some key thing that will allow him to move forward.

That old problem from Box 1 still exists, though, and we have to address it in the sixth and last section of the book. In *Lockdown*, the main character finds out whether or not he will get an early release from juvie. Even though there's not all that much riding on the decision (we know he's had a change of heart and will be okay either way), we still want to know the outcome.

Sometimes this section may be only a few pages long, or maybe just one page.

CHAPTER 13

FOR REAL?

The challenge in nonfiction writing is to make the narrative sound as interesting as possible, and not just to relate facts. If you are writing about a particular topic, chances are you are interested in it already. Think of what interests you about the topic specifically. What questions do you have? Where does your curiosity lead you?

Just like fiction, nonfiction should have a beginning, a middle, and an end. To give myself a structure, I approach nonfiction writing in the same way I do fiction: with an outline. Even if I am writing a one-page essay, I use this method. For nonfiction, my outline has four boxes instead of six.

FOUR-BOX MODEL FOR NONFICTION

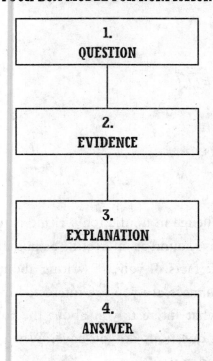

As with fiction, Box 1 is still the problem; but for nonfiction, I think of it as a question. I turn every essay into a question. So an essay on bullfighting becomes "Just How Brave Is the Matador?" This is not necessarily the title of the essay. The question allows me to organize the piece.

Box 2 is the evidence that supports the conclusion in Box 4. I need to collect evidence by doing research. I prefer to rely on primary sources, on conducting interviews, and on reading books, letters, and newspaper articles.

Box 3 is my explanation of why the evidence in Box 2 leads to the conclusion in Box 4. To stand within inches of the bull's flashing horns is brave; to know that others have died in the ring and still to fight is brave; to know the strength of the bull and still to fight is brave. Thus my conclusion in Box 4—that the matador is brave—has validity.

Box 4 is the answer to the question. Here I ask myself if I have really answered the question. Is my answer clear? Do I offer supportive evidence? Does the evidence really lead to my conclusion?

Biographies are a wonderful way to try your hand as a new writer. First of all, it's not too difficult to come up with a beginning, middle, and end to your story. (She was born, she had interests that moved her to do something significant, and she acted on those interests).

When I write a biography, I make two time lines. I do one on the life of the person I am writing about and another one that covers the significant news events that had an effect on that person, including what was going on during his or her lifetime. For example, Ida Wells was the daughter of a man who had been enslaved. Black people weren't treated well during her lifetime. Ida wrote about injustice. It was important for Ida's writings to play a central role in my brief biography of her. The fact that segregation was legal played an important part in her story. She objected to being told where she could sit on a train decades before Rosa Parks and the civil rights movement of the nineteen sixties.

When I write biographies, I spend days, sometimes months, filling in time lines. I go to the newspaper files in the public library and scroll through them to see what I might use to inform my reader of the significance of the subject.

I love writing about philosophy, too. But it's not always simple and easy to write nonfiction. In fact, it can be harder than fiction, because you're not just making things up. You have to take facts and make them interesting to a reader. While working on *All the Right Stuff*, I was drowning in an ocean of papers and books every day while I sorted through philosophical texts about social contract theory. On the next spread you can see some of the complex prewriting and thinking I did for the book.

One book that held particular meaning for me as a writer was a picture book I collaborated on with my son Christopher as the illustrator: *We Are America: A Tribute from the Heart*. After the 2001 terror attacks on the World Trade Center, I thought a lot about what it meant to me to be an American. We were all grieving together. Then there was a shift from grief to anger.

What came next surprised me and made me question my own identity as an American. There was a surge of patriotism and pride in our country after the events of 9/11. But what does it mean to be patriotic? How is patriotism defined? I heard a lot of people spouting their own definitions, but those didn't feel right for me.

I started to think of my relationship with America like I was a character in Box 4 of the fiction outline. I felt responsible for taking stock of America's past and present, figuring out what I wanted for America in the future, and working toward creating that future.

I used my own history as an American, and my feelings about what that meant. Looking at American

Social Contract

```
                              ┌─────────┐      ┌──────┐
                    ┌─────────│ Fairness│──────│ Race │
  ┌──────────────┐  │         │ as an   │      └──────┘
  │  Value of    │──┘         │ issue   │      ┌──────────┐
  │  Social      │            └─────────┘  ┌───│ Economic │
  │  Contract    │─────────────────────────┘   │ class    │
  └──────────────┘                             └──────────┘
                                               ┌───────────┐
                                           ┌───│ Knowledge │
                                           └   └───────────┘

  ┌──────────────┐   ┌──────────┐    ┌────────┐
  │ Altruist     │   │ Social   │────│ What   │
  │ Behavior     │───│ Contract │    │ is     │
  │              │   │          │    │ it?    │
  └──────────────┘   │          │    └────────┘
                     │          │    ┌────────┐
                     │          │────│ Sub    │
                     └──────────┘    │ Types  │
                          │          └────────┘
  ┌──────────────┐   ┌──────────────┐  ┌──────────┐
  │ Psychology   │   │ How to fulfill│──│ Traps-   │
  │ of the       │───│              │  │ Pitfalls │
  │ S. C.        │   │              │  └──────────┘
  └──────────────┘   └──────────────┘
        │                  │
  ┌──────────────┐   ┌──────────────┐
  │ Thinking     │   │ When: Time   │
  │              │   │ Concepts     │
  └──────────────┘   └──────────────┘
```

S.C. contd.

Thinking

Psychology of action

Dead vs Not Dead

Multiple Reasons to act

1. Not to feel bad
2. To feel good
3. To problem solve
4. Tribal advancement

history, I took from the past and reexamined documents and public statements. I allowed my own feelings to come into the writing. I started with history. I reread the Declaration of Independence, the Articles of Confederation, the Federalist Papers, and the Constitution—some of which I hadn't read since I was a teenager. I was reminded of the passion with which our country was created, a passion that would be universally inspirational and would be the model for governments all over the world. By making myself learn more about my country, I found that the writing of *We Are America* ended up being a journey not of discovery but of rediscovery. I worked out my truest feelings for my country through writing *We Are America*.

I love writing nonfiction because it offers these invaluable learning experiences, and also offers unique challenges to me as a writer. When you write nonfiction, you still need to do the same kind of work and planning you'd do for a fiction story. If you can learn enough about a topic to figure out how to present it in an exciting way, you'll not only grow as a writer, but also create a piece that is just as compelling to the reader as a work of fiction.

CHAPTER 14

CHECK IT OUT

Research goes hand in hand with reading in many ways. Just as reading extensively will expand your ideas of what is possible, it will probably pique your interest to find out more about a topic.

Research also goes hand in hand with writing. Of course, when you're writing nonfiction, you'll need to research your topic in depth, collecting evidence to fill your four-box outline. In fiction writing, you may also have to do research or verify details. Doing research is useful because it helps make your writing authentic. Even if you're writing fantasy, the supernatural world you create has a logic of its own. All the details need to be accurate and consistent.

Opposite is a notebook page of a list of topics that I wanted to research for my novel *Game*.

Sometimes it can work the opposite way, and research for its own sake can lead you to new projects. I am constantly becoming interested in various topics and will start looking into them innocently enough, only to have my curiosity rewarded with a bunch of ideas for new books.

When you're creating a whole world in your mind and on paper, there might be things you want to include that you don't know that much about. One example in my life was when I was cowriting *Kick*, whose teen character was a soccer player. I am a basketball player, so it was easy for me to imagine how the character would feel about playing a sport, wanting to win, and being disappointed if his team didn't win. I didn't know anything about soccer, though. I spoke with my co-author, Ross, who played soccer; watched some games; and picked up a copy of *Soccer for Dummies*.

While working on the same novel, Ross needed to write a chapter in which the main character was arrested and ended up potentially facing juvenile detention. Ross had never been arrested himself and didn't know exactly what happened in that situation.

Character (Cont'd)

He has a neighborhood.
   neighborhood — (photos)
He has primary understanding of his problems
   Problem
      Reflection

I don't want to internalize the problem too much.
   In a Walter Dean Myers — nothing happens

Carrier Problem
   Radio Wave Analogy

One problem that's cropping up today is that of European Ballplayers.

~~Drew — Iago and Othello~~

~~5 pps a day~~

               Research
            1. High School Games
            2. Sports magazines
               a) attention
               b) lies
               c) attention being paid
               d) bribes + money
            3. Prague
            4. Tomas' Background
            5. Othello + Iago
            6. Shakespeare
            7. Tony's failure

5 pps a day

He contacted a public defender who works with kids in juvie and set up an interview.

Another time, I decided to write a novel based in London. I was able to travel to London and went around photographing all the potential sites where the scenes in my novel might take place. This was an adult novel, and one aspect dealt with the stock market. I knew I had to do some research about the stock market, but I also knew that this was only a part of my book, not the focus. I wasn't as interested in replicating the stock market's atmosphere as I was in not making gross mistakes.

When you're doing research, you have to remember that the research has to serve the story, not the other way around. You have more leeway than you might think at first. It's helpful to stay focused on your book and the story you're trying to tell. You can pick and choose what to use and what to throw out.

My penchant for collecting antique photographs led me to write *Brown Angels*, a book designed like an antique photo album. The people featured are ordinary, everyday Americans, and the book shows that kids are alike—no matter when they lived. Another book of photographs, *Now Is Your Time!*, shows famous African Americans.

For a lot of the details in my books, I pull from my own memories. This is a great place to start, especially for young writers. I use memories from my days in Harlem, looking back at old photographs I have, and often researching to hone my details even further. (You can never do too much research.)

My wife and I spend part of each year in London. A used-book dealer there sold me a packet of letters from an African princess who had been a protégée of Queen Victoria in the mid-1800s. This piqued my interest and eventually led to my book *At Her Majesty's Request: An African Princess in Victorian England.*

Here's how I did my research for that project: The letters were written by Sarah Forbes Bonetta, who was a west African princess. I was fascinated the moment I began to read them, but it was difficult to take them out of the country, as some of Sarah's letters were correspondence with Queen Victoria herself! Once I had the letters in hand (after a bit of convincing), I spent a lot of time reading and rereading them. What I was interested in was what was going on between the lines. In her letters, the princess wrote like she didn't have a care in the world. As a young girl, though, she had almost been killed. Thinking of her as a character, I imagined what she would remember of her personal history, and of course how it affected her life.

I went through my library looking for clues and found a book written by Frederick E. Forbes, the captain who rescued the princess and took her to England in 1850. I felt as though my research was a bit of a wild-goose chase. I even went to Windsor Castle on another trip to London. I was ecstatic when I found a photo of the princess that was part of an exhibition in Ontario, Canada, on the internet.

Maybe part of what makes research so much fun is that it helps you to become a truly curious person. It's so exciting to wonder about something, go looking for the answer, and find it out. It's like solving a mystery and putting a puzzle together. It makes you wonder about more and more things, and believe that the truth is out there waiting to be discovered. Even after I wrote *At Her Majesty's Request*, I was still interested in Sarah Forbes Bonetta. On a trip to London long after I'd started writing the manuscript, I figured out in which hotel she'd spent her final days. I'll probably be researching her for the rest of my life.

While researching the history of cowboys, I found out that thirty percent of the cowboys in the American West were either African American or Mexican. This led me to write *The Journal of Joshua Loper: A Black*

Cowboy: The Chisholm Trail, 1871.

Other stories have come from experiences in my life. My younger brother, Thomas Wayne "Sonny" Myers, died in Vietnam in 1968, and I dedicated a book I wrote about the Vietnam War, *Fallen Angels*, to him.

The idea for *Fallen Angels* also came from something I'd already written. I wrote a short story about Sonny being killed in 'Nam, then a second story about what I had been doing in the army, and neither satisfied me completely. I had joined the army first, and then, some time later, my brother followed suit. I was miserable when his death was announced and felt compelled to write the story of all the young men of my generation who had fought and died in that bloody conflict. In *Fallen Angels*, a historical novel, I continued to explore my own thoughts about the war and my brother's death.

The best part of research is making it fit with your story. It really stimulates my imagination when I try to blend my own life experiences with new things I've found out through research.

Currently, I am researching the Normandy invasion of 1944. The veterans I speak with are now elderly, but all are still emotional about the invasion and most are eager to have their stories told. I try to have at least two sessions with each subject I interview. During the first interview, I introduce myself and ask a fixed number of questions, including whether I can be granted a follow-up interview if I think of more questions. The second session is always more useful, because the person I interview has had a chance to rethink the events and come up with even more stories.

While I love history and uncovering rare sources of information, the vast majority of my books come directly from my observations of the young people I write about. I tend to write a lot about teens who are troubled as I was growing up. When I visit kids in schools, libraries, and juvenile detention centers, I listen to them talk about their experiences and even ask them what they want me to write about. In the meantime, I also encourage them to write their stories. Hopefully, if we keep working together, there will be fewer stories like theirs in years to come.

CHAPTER 15

Discipline

As a teenager I wrote longhand in composition books. I filled up book after book with never a revision and few changes. When I began writing again as an adult, I wrote when I felt like it, or when someone asked me to. I didn't expect to get paid much for my writing, and that certainly was the case. Sometimes my only payment was free copies of the magazine or journal that was publishing me. But there were other rewards. One day I was playing basketball in a Brooklyn playground, and during a break one of the players said that he had come across a remarkable thing.

"I read a story in *Liberator* magazine, and it was about basketball and *this* park!" he said. "I couldn't believe it!"

He produced the magazine and started showing it around. It was my story. What a thrill to have the guys I hung out with gathered around, reading my story. It made me feel really good about myself.

But I knew a lot of young people who wanted to be, or called themselves, writers. Some of them wrote very well. I was publishing stories in small magazines, and a few newspaper articles, and had actually found a job as an editor with a major publisher. What I noted, among my friends and other younger writers, was that the biggest difficulty most of them had was not in the quality of their writing but in their ability to finish a project. As I talked to dozens of writers, I reached the conclusion that most of them, when they sat down to write, came up with a variation of the "genius" theory. Shakespeare was a "genius," Dickens was a "genius," as were Shelley, Keats, Hesse, Camus, etc. Any writer worth his or her salt had the stamp of genius and therefore didn't have to work at writing. So when I decided I wanted to try to make a living as a writer, I knew I needed to find a way of finishing books, not just starting them.

The first thing I did was to decide that I would write eight hours a day. If bus drivers worked eight hours a day (do they?), then I would do the same and call it my "job." But I knew I wouldn't be typing eight hours a day, so what would be my "job" during the other hours? If I watched television, looking for ideas, would that be a good thing? How about if I took a lot of naps waiting for inspiration? What I decided was that I would write ten pages a day. And I did, for the first three years that I was a stay-at-home writer. I wrote ten pages a day and usually threw away between three and six.

I cut my writing to five pages a day. Five pages a day, five days a week. What would I do with the other hours in the day? I would think about structure, and about my characters. How would I force myself to do the thinking on balmy June days when I wanted to go play ball? I would do outlines.

My workday goes like this: I'm up between four thirty and five a.m. I feed our cat, Sheba, read the online newspapers, and then start work. My goal for the day is five pages. I might take four hours to write the pages, or less than an hour. When I finish the five pages, I stop typing, save my work, and congratulate myself.

Even if I'm hot and the writing is going really well, I resist the urge to continue. I know my brain will continue to work, continue to enrich the material, and I'll have an easier start the next morning.

CHAPTER 16

LEAVE YOUR EGO AT THE DOOR

When you have completed your book and you think it's ready for publication, it can be incredibly helpful to find a reader. You've probably been your own reader many times by now as you've completed the drafts. You've gone back and forth, trying different ideas. You've probably changed details in earlier chapters as you've learned more and more about your characters through the writing process. Maybe you've figured out that one of your initial ideas wasn't as great as something you thought of later, and you've changed some aspects of the story around. Maybe after doing some research, you've found places where you need to make alterations to keep your story accurate.

You can really improve your writing skills as your own reader and editor, but there are some limitations when self-editing. Think about the world of your book. It all exists in your head. You've created so many details. Only a part of the story is on paper. The rest is in your head, and it's difficult to read your own work without filling in the blanks.

Find a reader who has never met your characters or entered your imagined world. Ask people you know if they would like to read your story. It should be some-one you trust and respect. (If you don't respect them, why would you care what they say about your writ-ing? It won't make you a better writer to throw their opinions out the window.) Maybe a family member, a friend, or a teacher would be willing to give you honest feedback on your story.

It's still up to you to decide if the criticism is good or not. If it gives you something to think about, to con-sider, by all means do the thinking. You don't have to agree with someone just because that person has some supposed authority. Writing, in the end, is a solitary endeavor, and you must, in the end, rely upon your own judgment.

Now comes the hard part. I'm used to getting long,

complicated letters from my editors. (I think editors love to write long, complicated letters.) For me, it's just part of the process. But it's never easy to have someone question and poke and prod your work. I've been doing this for years, and sometimes my first reaction will still be outrage. You write "the class gasped when Jennifer entered the room." You're astounded that your editor should ask you why the class gasped. Of course anyone would fully expect the class to gasp when they saw Jennifer enter the room stark naked and eating an orange. Calm down a little bit; go back and reread what you've written. You'll find that the bit about the orange and the no clothes didn't make it from your head to the paper. Oops.

Usually, I will sit down and read the editor's whole letter and look at all the comments and the questions I've been asked. I'll read it once all the way through, and then I'll just sit and think about it for a little while. After the initial shock has worn off, I'll usually start to feel the editor is right about a lot of things. Maybe a day or so afterward, I'll go through the manuscript page by page, rewriting and revising to address most everything my editor has pointed out.

Keep in mind, though, that your editor is not always right. What you don't want to do is just go through and mindlessly make changes based on what your reader recommends. Instead, look closely at the reader's questions and comments. Consider them one by one and decide whether you feel they are justified or not.

When you disagree on something, that can be useful, too. If there's something your reader doesn't understand, it means you as a writer haven't done a good enough job of getting it across. Forge on! The result will be well worth it. You'll end up with clean, crisp writing that is an improvement over what you started out with. You'll know that what you want to say is coming across. That's sort of the whole point, isn't it?

CHAPTER 17

Hey, Get Back Here

I am not usually that conscious of the act of daydreaming, and first drafts for me are close to automatic writing. The second draft is where the real writing begins for me.

By the time you are rewriting and revising, you probably know the characters in your book as if they were real people. Maybe you've been able to find a reader to give you some ideas about where you need to add more details. By revising and rewriting, you will get more of the essential story onto the paper.

Also, you've grown over the life of the book. Some things that you wrote at the beginning of the book just don't work by the time you get to the end! If the story is well constructed, revising is quite enjoyable. I've heard people claim that revisions are tedious and boring, but I can't imagine feeling that way. A real writer will love this part of the process. This is your chance to bring what you've learned about your characters into every scene.

Sometimes I have my wife, an artist, look over the manuscript and see where I can fit in descriptions. I've noticed over the years that my books have a tendency to take place in my characters' minds, and I often overlook what the setting is like. When my wife points out places I could describe, I'll go back to see if those places actually need a description. She's usually right.

When Ross Workman and I were writing *Kick*, writing the final chapter took the longest time. This was because we both had become engrossed in rewriting and revising the rest of the book. A lot of time has probably gone by in your life between the day you started thinking about your book and today, when you are beginning to write your final chapter. You may have had experiences that have changed you or taught you new things, and you may want to incorporate your own new perspective into the story. Maybe you've met someone who has inspired you.

Some famous writers say they don't like to rewrite because it ruins the spontaneity of their work. Unfortunately, this shows in the work. In my experience, the freedom and drama of the spontaneous pieces only show up once in a while. Most of the time, everything can use a rewrite.

Don't be too hard on yourself during your rewrite, though. Enjoy your writing. This should be fun, not a chore. One of the things I've learned over the years is to be careful not to take out the good stuff when I'm rewriting.

Once you've had a reader give you some feedback, you'll need to figure out a plan for revising. Go back to your outline. Are there kinks you need to work out in the story arc? The story arc is the link that takes the story from page one to page whatever. Maybe when you first put the plot together, you were a bit cautious because you didn't know your characters. Now you have a better idea of who they are and who you are as a writer. Remember, the stronger you can make your story arc, the easier the writing will be. Go back and rework your outline chapter by chapter to incorporate the new plot elements.

Then go back a chapter at a time for your revisions and rewriting, adding in the things you've altered in your outline. Some chapters might require extensive rewriting and others very little.

CHAPTER 18

THERE'S ROOM ON THIS PAGE
FOR THE BOTH OF US

Writing with a coauthor can be incredibly informative and rewarding. You can each help develop the other's writing. You'll have a partner to bounce ideas off when you're doing your thinking about the story and characters. And you'll only have to do half the work! (Just kidding.)

There are a number of ways to collaborate on a book, and I've tried a few of them. My first effort, a mystery-adventure book with a close friend, ended the friendship. I was accused of being an egomaniac, a rotter, and a know-it-all. I haven't spoken to my former friend for over twenty-five years.

A second effort involved another friend (my way of culling friends?). The plan at the outset was that he'd do the research and I would do the writing. What ended up happening was that I did most of the research, too.

In my entire career, I have participated in only one writing collaboration that I would call a success. That book was *Kick*. Ross and I started "kicking" around ideas in 2007. The book was published in 2011. See? I'm serious when I say it takes a lot of time and hard work to write.

All writing projects interest me, but in this case the project took me by surprise; I hadn't been thinking about a collaboration.

One of the most valuable things I learned from working with Ross was that his interest in the writing process was what would carry the book through to completion. On reexamining my own writing career and trying to compare my thirteen-to-fifteen-year-old efforts to what Ross was accomplishing, I could see what we had in common: we both loved the process of creating stories. Just like you.

Ross is very bright. Whenever he made what seemed to be a misstep, I would examine his text to see why. Sometimes I would note just a lack of experience in a certain area or a willingness to accept the first idea he had rather than look for a better one. But once shown the weakness in a passage or chapter, he would tackle the rewrite willingly and, mostly, successfully.

I think I taught Ross to be open to criticism. We had to deal with an editor who wanted the best book possible and has no qualms about criticizing me. I've known many writers, old and young, who can't accept that sometimes they will have to work very hard to create a good piece of literature. In soccer terms, I would consider Ross "highly coachable."

When I began my collaboration with Ross, I did it with some trepidation and a lot of surprise. It was only when the book reached the final prepublication stages that I began to ask myself why I had been attracted to working with a young man barely in his teens. The answer became apparent once I had reread our original email conversations. We were almost immediately chatting about the work at hand and not about each other.

I love being a writer. I love sitting at the computer (or with my notebook in bed), making up stories and exploring the lives of my characters. Ross got this immediately. One day we were talking about the possibility of writing together; the next, we were talking about plot and characters, and shortly thereafter, the book began to happen. We had, in effect, found the common ground of the writing process itself.

Our few disagreements were about the elements of the book, not about our individual ego needs. A successful writer needs the ability to see his work as a separate entity apart from himself.

The most important aspect of a successful collaboration is that both authors are willing to work hard. Ross was diligent. He sent me his character time line and his ideas for the book's outline. But I knew Ross was a writer only after he sent me his first chapter.

The picture books I do with my son Christopher and other artists are also collaborations, as the writer and illustrator interact with each other's concepts. Writers don't normally have long discussions with the artists who illustrate their books. Writing a picture book often means a lot of waiting anxiously to see what a particular illustrator has made of your work. With Christopher, I do get feedback through the woman I live with, who just happens to be his mother.

CHAPTER 19

PICK YOURSELF UP, DUST YOURSELF OFF

Maybe you have heard the term "writer's block." I don't necessarily believe in writer's block, because I think writing will come if the writer has taken the time to do some very good prethinking before beginning a book. Sometimes, I feel "writer's block" is an excuse. It usually means that the writer didn't spend enough time planning the book and has gotten lost along the way.

That said, I do believe that something that commonly happens to writers is a loss of confidence. There are things you can look out for in your own writing that might show that you are not feeling so great about yourself as a writer. A reader is only going to continue reading because he or she wants to discover (not merely be told) what the central character is thinking and, more important, feeling. Look out for telling versus showing. Telling is lazy writing that doesn't reward the reader. Readers want to feel they are discovering new things about the character throughout the novel.

If you are feeling frustrated while writing, like you just want to get on to the next paragraph and explain the next thing, take a break. Go back and reread what you've written. Are you letting the story develop on the page naturally? Are you describing events and the actions of your character and letting the reader make inferences as to how the character is feeling and changing? Or are you doing too much telling?

Losing confidence is something that happens to all of us at times. I've always written quickly, which makes people think I don't have problems with the writing. Actually, I have a stack of unpublished manuscripts that are evidence of my drifting off into la-la land—not being sure of what I was writing about or (as sometimes happens when I set out to write "great literature") allowing the writing to get in the way of the story. I save them in hopes that one day I'll be able to see whatever it was I thought I was doing.

I've seen writers I greatly admire completely blow it. Writers try to pretend that it's easier than it is. It's about the work. It's about taking risks and seeing what works and cutting what doesn't and challenging yourself to keep trying even while knowing you might fail.

I believe that your skills as a writer are not so much defined by intelligence or artistic ability as they are by how much of yourself you are willing to bring to the page. Be brave. You know how to write. You know how to finish a book.

Try to remind yourself that you're good enough to do this. You can make it happen.

CHAPTER 20

WRITING IS GOOD FOR YOU

Writing can change the writer.

Did I tell you I love what I do? Did I tell you that every day I have a creative experience that makes me more than I could imagine ever being? Did I tell you that the boy in me wants to write the stories that I wanted desperately to read as a teenager? Did I tell you that the stories I write are my way of merging my own small universe with that of my readers and that this is my way of celebrating this wondrous gift of life?

Ultimately, I want my books to be not only portals to other books, and to other cultures, but also pathways from the unforgiving geography that we so passively accept, to the far reaches of every lonely and despairing heart. I hope to offer the discomforts of conscience, and the pleasures of rediscovering our humanity.

I was on a subway in New York when I saw a young girl reading a book of mine, *Monster*. That's quite a thrill in itself, but after turning a few pages she stopped reading, closed the book, and for a few moments was lost in thought. She had taken my words and run off with them to her own private place. In that moment all our boundaries—age, gender, race— had been bridged. If I had been dead, it wouldn't have mattered, for on that page, in that rocking train, even mortality had been put aside. How beautiful a moment for a boy from Harlem who loved to read.

I am grateful for book lovers all over the world. I am grateful for those who teach books and read- ing and who understand what books can mean and who understood enough about me when I was a boy to bring me to this process. I am grateful for you, an aspiring writer of the books we'll all read tomorrow.

CHAPTER 21

WHO ARE YOU?

We've talked about the many challenges we face as writers. But what about those we face as people? Good writing means evolving. Can I continue to grow as an individual and therefore as an artist?

Just as characters gain insight, grow, and change, so do writers. Writing a book will make you think about the world in a different way. Hopefully, if you were interested in writing to begin with, the tools in this book have helped you to develop your passion.

Writing is mostly a matter of interpreting the work as a craft. We constantly learn how to do it better and what works and what doesn't work. Making sure I'm consistently challenging myself to grow as an individual is trickier.

I do this by focusing on the things I feel passionate about. One of those is staying connected with young people, and with young people in the juvenile justice system in particular.

In a 2005 Supreme Court case, *Roper v. Simmons*, it was decided that a kid under the age of eighteen could not be executed for a crime other than homicide. It was a very close five-to-four decision, very hotly contested. In 2010, the Supreme Court was considering whether a minor could be given a sentence of life in prison without the possibility of parole. Because the case in 2005 had been so controversial, I certainly did not expect the court to rule against life without parole for minors. I was surprised and hopeful when the court ruled in a six-to-three vote to bar a minor from a life sentence without the possibility of parole, unless the crime was a homicide. I didn't think they were going to go for it.

I believe that all kids who commit crimes deserve a second chance. I do not think you can look at a kid who's fourteen, fifteen, or sixteen years old and say, "This kid has to be thrown away." This is a human being. And if we respect ourselves as human beings, we have to respect these kids. We know where they're coming from. We know their environment. We know what the pressures are to participate in some of these crimes. And we understand that given some maturity, given some opportunity, the kids in question can change and better themselves.

I believe this sincerely, and so it permeates my writing.

These kids very often don't even know what a crime is. They do things, and they have an idea of justice. They might do something that, in their mind, isn't "so bad," without knowing what will happen to them, legally, if they get caught. I see this all the time. Sometimes kids will even get bullied into participating in a crime. Maybe they just carry something from one place to another. But according to the law, that lands you in jail. The kids are shocked. I actually have interviewed kids who never knew they were going to jail, because now jails are called "Horizons" or "Bridges" or "Progress," which is the name of the facility in my novel *Lockdown*. They have these nice names, and then the kids find they're locked up, thrown away.

I am disturbed by this, and so it shows up in my books.

I think it's tough for juvenile detention facilities to

really help rehabilitate kids. It's part of the process of the kids' parole and release to go back to the same environment. They go right back to the same things that got them into juvie in the first place.

I can't stop the kids or, by myself, change the system, so I write about it with all the intensity that I can muster.

I visit them because I find some of them connecting with my work. I feel we have to reach out and talk to these kids. I tell them I was raised in Harlem. I was a high school dropout. I needed something in my life to tell me I was okay. I was secretly saying to myself, "Walter, you're crap." I needed something, and I wish I could have found the book. I wish I'd found that story when I was fourteen or fifteen.

I believe we can help these kids. We have to give them a voice. We have to give them language. We have to say to them, "Look. I know you're mad at society, but you can't be mad at yourself. You can't give up trying." We have to have elevated conversations with these kids. We have to tell them, "Okay, this is what life is about." These kids don't know. We have to tell them, "You can't hate yourself anymore. You have to reach within yourself, because no one is going to do it for you."

While I was writing *Lockdown*, I reread *Man's Search for Meaning* by Viktor E. Frankl. Frankl was talking about people in concentration camps, and how they had to come out of themselves, stop hating themselves, and find something outside themselves to love.

I was once running on a track on New York's Lower East Side when I saw another runner wearing a pretty blue jumpsuit. I assumed that his lack of "real sweats" meant that he couldn't run. I challenged him by running up on him and giving him a semi-mean mug, and he ignored me. Then I ran up again and gestured toward him to really run. At last he shrugged, waited until we were abreast, and took off. I mean, the dude could fly! He left me behind as if I had been standing still.

Afterward, I found that it was Dick Gregory, a civil rights activist but also a former nationally ranked miler. I was kind of sucking up to him and asked him how much he ran currently. He said he ran three miles a day when he was fasting (gasp!) and six miles when he wasn't fasting. When I suggested that his schedule was amazing, he said it wasn't, that running only took two hours of his time every day. "If you can't spend two hours a day doing something for yourself," he said, "then what are you living for?"

It got me to thinking about my use of time and the question in general. Few of us spend time doing something for ourselves. Let's belong to that group.

Now You're a Writer
by Ross Workman

I've always had many interests, and one of those interests is writing. In first grade, I wrote and illustrated a book about my first-grade teacher . . . who had superpowers. I was always most interested in the creative writing in English class and often did extra work on the assignments. I found that I learned more from assignments in which we had to rewrite the endings of novels we were reading for class than from answering questions about the content and meaning of books. You have to understand a story, each character, and what the author intended in order to create a believable new ending for it.

I've also always been an avid reader, especially of nonfiction on a wide variety of subjects. Some of the subjects I have enjoyed reading about are World Wars I and II, the Civil War, geography, and ancient and medieval history. In order to be a writer, you also have to be a reader.

I have been a fan of Walter Dean Myers's books since first reading *Scorpions* in fifth grade. His books opened a new world for me. I didn't feel that I was like any of the characters he wrote about, but I could relate to and sympathize with them. They seemed like kids I could be friends with. *Fallen Angels*, *Monster*, *It Ain't All for Nothing*, *Shooter*, *Handbook for Boys*, and *Game* became my favorite books.

Walter was the first author I'd ever written to. I just had to tell him how much his books meant to me. I wanted him to know that I loved his books and thought he was the best writer around because he really connected with kids. When I wrote him a fan letter at the age of thirteen, the last thing I expected was that he would write back and ask me to write a book with him. But that's what happened. At first I wasn't sure if Walter was joking, but once I realized he was serious, I wrote back to say of course I'd write a book with him! At thirteen, I didn't know if I'd be any good at writing a book, but I was going to try my best.

I started by asking Walter a lot of questions: "What is the main character's neighborhood like? What city or state will he live in? What point of view will the story be written in? What is his home situation?" I quickly learned that I would have to answer these questions myself! That's an important part of being a writer.

Walter suggested that I make a time line of the life of the main character (whom I named Kevin), outlining each year of his life from birth to the present with a paragraph. That way, I would really know who Kevin was. I also had to invent secondary characters, such as Kevin's soccer teammates and his family. Walter also gave me a tip for a way to visualize my characters. One of his techniques is finding pictures of what his characters look like in magazines or newspapers and cutting them out and posting them on the wall above his computer. I used this method, and it certainly helped. It gave me a mental image of all the characters, and it helped me not only with character development and keeping my character's appearance consistent, but also in imagining the setting and the way the characters interacted.

Walter quickly sent me a letter reacting to my character profile, time line, and plot suggestions, with great feedback. I did some revision on the time line and plot summary, and then Walter wrote the first chapter and sent it to me. It was terrific.

Now it was time for me to write chapter two. Writing it wasn't easy. I said to Walter, "This has been one of the most enjoyable things I've ever done, and also one of the hardest." The chapter takes place in a juvenile correctional facility, a place I've never been. Before I wrote, I called a lawyer my family knew to get some background information about what goes on in juvenile detention centers, and I did some research. Walter explained that research should really serve the writing, not the other way around. It wasn't a fantastic chapter, but I got an amazing response from Walter:

"Now I know you're a writer."

Those were some of the best words I'd ever read.

I imagined that we would now continue to write the book. However, Walter suggested that I first prepare an outline. I was a little surprised to be doing an outline, since that was how I learned to write essays and papers in my English classes, but not how I learned to write fiction. But the outline would help give the story much-needed structure and focus. And writing an outline keeps a writer from getting stuck in the middle of a book and not finishing. Walter explained that what we wrote in the outline would be tentative. That seemed fine to me, and I was interested to see how the story would develop. Walter's chapters—and even my own—could take very surprising turns.

Kevin, the main character in *Kick*, is very different from me and everyone I know. He's hotheaded: he gets into fights and doesn't always think before he acts. And even though it's easy to let your personality seep into the mind of your character, I had to make sure he always acted and sounded like Kevin, and not like me.

The chapters in my first draft of *Kick* were set in my town. In the revisions, I took out the references to places in my own town and made the town entirely fictitious. I have to admit I don't have quite as clear a picture of the town now as I did when it was my own, but I thought the setting should be invented, which is actually a little harder to do. You have to completely imagine a new place.

It goes without saying that life experiences help a writer. I think it's hard to write well in a vacuum. I found that other parts of my life—reading, interacting with friends, participating in sports, and even playing music—helped me become a better creative writer. The sports helped me with my soccer scenes and made them more realistic. Interactions with my peers at school helped me write social scenes and develop more believable characters. Even musical training helped me to be a better writer. I play the saxophone. So much of what a writer does, especially in the first draft, involves improvising. Sometimes you have to keep the pace of the story fast, like a rapid saxophone solo, and sometimes you have to slow it down so the reader can stop to think.

As a teenager, I have found it easier to write based on my life experiences than to imagine a life that is entirely different from my own. I hope that will change in my writing as I get older and have more experience. Some of the writing was particularly difficult for me, especially dialogue between Kevin and his close female friend, Christy. When it came time to write dialogue between a boy and a girl, I faltered. I just didn't know a lot of girls when I was thirteen and fourteen! I wrote to Walter about the difficulty, and he responded: "Why do you think all my novels are told from the male's point of view?!"

More than a year after our first correspondence, Walter and I met in person. I was extremely nervous about meeting him. I was invited by Walter's editor at HarperCollins, Phoebe Yeh, to visit the company to talk about the book together and to have lunch. The meeting in the HarperCollins offices was great, and it was thrilling to finally meet Walter Dean Myers after reading his books for so many years and then working with him for a year. Phoebe discussed her terrific revision ideas with us at the meeting and in a letter she sent to us after the meeting. There was no sense of whether or not the book would be published at this point, but Phoebe was willing to work with us. I was a little apprehensive about whether I would be able to do what she asked, but I wanted to give my best effort. I wouldn't want anyone to read my work unless I thought it was the best it could be.

The revision process was in a lot of ways more difficult than writing the first draft, and it took even longer—about two years—to complete. Sometimes I got discouraged while revising a chapter, because I felt as though what I wrote in eighth grade wasn't good, or wasn't up to the level of what I was now capable of writing in high school. This is where I had the most difficulty: while revising, I felt my style of writing was constantly changing along with my age, and had changed from the initial time when Walter and I had been writing and exchanging chapters. But I'd have been more worried if my writing hadn't developed, now that I was older and knew more about writing.

On the positive side, I had lived with the characters long enough to know who they really were and to flesh out their lives in my mind. I also had a better sense of what was and what wasn't working. I had to be very careful, now that I was older, to keep Kevin sounding thirteen. His speech and personality couldn't age or grow along with me.

In the revision process, I hit a few bumps. After I rewrote chapter two pretty drastically, Walter responded that I'd tried to fix too much right away, and I needed to revert to my first effort. "One of the things that I've learned over the years," he said, "is that when I'm doing a rewrite, I must be careful not to take out the good stuff." I had tremendous trouble with chapter eight, and Walter was disappointed with the revision. I was unhappy with it myself. I was experiencing something that most writers go through: I had lost confidence in myself. Especially when I read Walter's chapters, I felt I could never measure up and be the great writer he is. I was lucky to have a mentor to help me out of this situation. Walter said: "Don't worry about losing confidence—it happens to all of us at times. It's about the work, Ross. It's about trial and error and putting yourself out there to possibly fail at times. We will make it happen."

Walter is very kind but is not effusive with his praise. What he says he really means, and because of this, his words bear infinitely more weight than the average person's. His amazing personality also translates into his writing. Every sentence and word he writes is there for a purpose. He doesn't ramble and never says too much, making his books more thought-provoking and meaningful.

Walter and Phoebe patiently and kindly guided me through the process, and finally one day I was able to hold a copy of *Kick* in my hands! The jacket, which shows the shadow of a boy holding a soccer ball, is perfect, and it's a great metaphor for writing and reading. It does not give the reader a clear picture of Kevin but allows the reader room for imagination. That is what a book is all about. There is a story and plot and description, but much of a book leaves holes for the reader to fill in with his or her imagination. Unlike watching TV or a movie, the experience of reading a book will never be the same for any two people.

Getting to write a book with Walter Dean Myers was a once-in-a-lifetime experience. Not only did I learn a great deal about writing, but I also learned about the complicated process of making a book. The creative aspect is by far the most fun and exciting part.

But if you don't follow through and put words on paper, no one will ever see your work. Learning to love the process is as important as the passion of writing down those first words. The same energy needs to be applied to revising as when you excitedly wrote those first words of your novel.

Since *Kick* was published, I have continued to write. I always keep a notebook with me to jot down interesting thoughts that I can include in my writing. If I don't have a notebook, I write them in a notes section in my phone. And although I'm very busy with school, I make time to write on weekends, and I've been slowly working on another novel. But most writers write every day.

I will be off to college in the fall of 2012, and although I won't be majoring in creative writing, I definitely plan to take writing courses. In order to have material to write about, I think I need to learn about many other subjects and have diverse experiences.

Five years ago, I could not have imagined I would have published a book. Since you are already reading this book, you are way ahead of where I was when I started. Maybe you, too, will have your book published. Don't give up!

Top Ten Writing Tips from Walter Dean Myers

1. You don't need permission to be a writer. Just start doing it.
2. To write well, you have to know what good writing is. For me, this means reading good literature on a regular basis.
3. The time I spend prewriting usually predicts whether I will sell the book or not. The time I spend rewriting usually predicts the success of the book.
4. If the problem in your story or essay is crystal clear in your mind, the writing will be infinitely easier.
5. Anyone who loves the process of writing—creating characters, exploring the logic of a story or argument, and using language to convey thoughts and feelings—can become a successful writer.

6. Writer's block is not a matter of having nothing to write. It's a matter of not having given the project sufficient thought.

7. I can write a better twenty-page story if I write five pages a day for four days rather than writing twenty pages at one time.

8. Learn how to accept criticism of your work. It will make you a better writer.

9. If, starting at the age of fourteen, you write two good pages per day for five days each week, you'll probably be rich and famous by the time you're twenty-five. Okay, maybe twenty-seven.

10. Push yourself to continually expand your own horizons. Challenge yourself as an individual to keep your mind and heart open to new growth experiences.

Five Writing Tips from Ross Workman

1. While you're writing, it's helpful to have a thesaurus handy. I use one when I'm trying to think of a better word, or a better way to say something.
2. If you're writing in the first person, make sure your narrator sounds consistent. I had to be very careful about that, as I wrote my parts of *Kick* from the point of view of a thirteen-year-old boy. Whatever point of view you're using, keep in mind that it should always sound like the same person.
3. Don't permanently delete sections of your manuscript that you don't like. Put them either in a separate file or at the bottom of your manuscript, which is what I do. You never know when you might want to use some of what you wrote.
4. Be willing to revise as many times as it takes.
5. It's okay to make mistakes!

Suggestions for Further Reading

Fletcher, Ralph. *How to Write Your Life Story.* New York: HarperCollins, 2007.

———. *How Writers Work: Finding a Process That Works for You.* New York: HarperCollins, 2000.

———. *Live Writing: Breathing Life into Your Words.* New York: Avon, 1999.

———. *A Writer's Notebook: Unlocking the Writer within You.* New York: HarperCollins: 1996.

King, Stephen. *On Writing: A Memoir of the Craft.* New York: Scribner's, 2000.

Lamott, Anne. *Bird by Bird: Some Instructions on Writing and Life.* New York: Pantheon, 1994.

Levine, Gail Carson. *Writing Magic: Creating Stories that Fly.* New York: HarperCollins, 2006.

Welty, Eudora. *One Writer's Beginnings.* Cambridge, MA: Harvard University Press, 1983, 1984.

MEET THE AUTHOR

Critically acclaimed author Walter Dean Myers has garnered much respect and admiration for his fiction, nonfiction, and poetry for young people. In 1969, he won a Council on Interracial Books for Children contest, which resulted in the publication of his first book, *Where Does the Day Go?* Since then, he has become one of the most award-winning and prolific authors for young people, with over a hundred books to his credit.

Walter Dean Myers has won the Coretta Scott King Award five times (more than any author in the history of the award), has been awarded two Newbery Honors, and has won two National Book Award Honors. His book *Monster* was the winner of the first Michael L. Printz Award, a National Book Award Finalist, and a *New York Times* bestseller. *Monster* is required reading on the New York City public schools' eighth-grade curriculum, and *Now Is Your Time!*, a Coretta Scott King Award winner, is used to teach African American history. Walter Dean Myers received the Margaret A. Edwards Award for significant and lasting contribution to young adult literature; was selected to deliver the 2009 May Hill Arbuthnot Honor Lecture, a distinction reserved for an individual who has made significant contributions to the field of children's literature; and was the 2010 United States nominee for the Hans Christian Andersen Award, the highest international recognition given to an author of children's books. He is the first recipient of the Virginia Hamilton Award for Lifetime Achievement and the 2012–2013 National Ambassador for Young People's Literature.

A self-proclaimed "bad boy," Walter Dean Myers was raised in a foster home in Harlem, New York City, which is the setting of many of his books. He attended the prestigious Stuyvesant High School but dropped out just before his seventeenth birthday, when he joined the army. One of his teachers knew he was planning to leave school and told him to keep writing no matter what happened to him. She said, "It's what you do." Sure enough, years later, he began writing again about the most difficult period of his life, his teens. Writing for Myers has been a way to reach out to the world, establishing his humanity in a culture that often ignores the humanity of those in less favored positions.

"I want to humanize the people I depict," Myers says. "I want to show them struggling, yes. To show them living within their own cultural heritage, yes. But even more, I want to show them in the universal setting for love and meaning that we all experience."

Walter Dean Myers uses his own life experience, as well as meticulous research carried out during time spent in playgrounds, classrooms, youth detention centers, and prisons, as inspiration for his writing and to provide a discerning and uncompromising perspective on hard-hitting issues facing young people today. Leonard Marcus, in an article for the *New York Times*, wrote, "Drugs, drive-by shootings, gang warfare, wasted lives—Myers has written about all these subjects with nuanced understanding and a hard-won, qualified sense of hope." Myers's pioneering urban novels explore the decisions and values of young people and help readers expand their inner landscape and geography.

Walter Dean Myers is a frequent visitor to juvenile detention facilities. A foster child and high school dropout himself, he has a commitment to underserved children, often wondering, "Why not me?" He speaks with kids about everything from writing to second chances. Jessica Fenster-Sparber, library coordinator at Passages Academy in the Bronx, New York, says, "Students have told me if it weren't for his books, they would not read."

Many of Walter Dean Myers's books focus on mentoring, and he works with young writers to help them develop the skills to depict their experiences through the written word. In 2011, HarperCollins Children's Books released Myers's first published collaboration with a teen author, Ross Workman: their novel, *Kick*.

"A common thought among teens is that their problems are unique," Myers says. "When they discover, in a novel or biography, people facing the same issues, they begin to understand a lot more about the world they live in. Life can be hard; literature can help."

Myers understands the power that books hold. He employs literature as a bridge to self-value for children and young adults alike, combating negative attitudes and stereotypes. His extraordinary body of work includes picture books, poetry, screenplays, historical fiction, and more—celebrating and depicting the beauty, struggle, and pride of a people, a culture, and a place.

"When I was growing up, there weren't really any books by African Americans available," Myers says. "A turning point for me was the discovery of a short story by James Baldwin about the black urban experience. It gave me permission to write about my own experiences. And I'm still typing. . . ."

Walter Dean Myers lives in Jersey City, New Jersey.

ALL MY BOOKS . . . SO FAR

All the Right Stuff. New York: HarperCollins, 2012.

The Cruisers Book 2: Checkmate. New York: Scholastic, 2011.

We Are America: A Tribute from the Heart. Illustrated by Christopher Myers. New York: HarperCollins, 2011.

Carmen. New York: Egmont, 2011.

Kick. Coauthored by Ross Workman. New York: HarperCollins, 2011.

Looking for the Easy Life. Illustrated by Lee Harper. New York: HarperCollins, 2011.

Looking Like Me. Illustrated by Christopher Myers. New York: Egmont, 2010.

The Cruisers Book 1. New York: Scholastic, 2010.

Lockdown. New York: HarperCollins, 2010.

Muhammad Ali: The People's Champion. Illustrated by Alix Delinois. New York: HarperCollins, 2010.

Riot. New York: Egmont, 2009.

Amiri and Odette: A Love Story. Illustrated by Javaka Steptoe. New York: Scholastic, 2009.

Dope Sick. New York: HarperCollins, 2009.

Game. New York: HarperCollins, 2008.

Ida B. Wells: Let the Truth Be Told. Illustrated by Bonnie Christensen. New York: HarperCollins, 2008.

Sunrise over Fallujah. New York: Scholastic, 2008.

Harlem Summer. New York: Scholastic, 2007.

What They Found: Love on 145th Street. New York: Random House, 2007.

Harlem Hellfighters: When Pride Met Courage. New York: HarperCollins, 2006.

Jazz. Illustrated by Christopher Myers. New York: Holiday House, 2006.

Street Love. New York: HarperCollins, 2006.

Autobiography of My Dead Brother. Illustrated by Christopher Myers. New York: HarperCollins, 2005.

Antarctica: Journeys to the South Pole. New York: Scholastic, 2004.

Here in Harlem: Poems in Many Voices. New York: Holiday House, 2004.

I've Seen the Promised Land: The Life of Dr. Martin Luther King, Jr. Illustrated by Leonard Jenkins. New York: HarperCollins, 2004.

Shooter. New York: HarperCollins, 2004.

USS Constellation: Pride of the American Navy. New York: Holiday House, 2004.

The Beast. New York: Scholastic, 2003.

Blues Journey. Illustrated by Christopher Myers. New York: Holiday House, 2003.

The Dream Bearer. New York: HarperCollins, 2003.

A Time to Love: Stories from the Old Testament. Illustrated by Christopher Myers. New York: Scholastic, 2003.

Handbook for Boys: A Novel. New York: HarperCollins, 2002.

Patrol: An American Soldier in Vietnam. Illustrated by Ann Grifalconi. New York: Harper Collins, 2002.

Three Swords for Granada. Illustrated by John Speirs. New York: Holiday House, 2002.

Bad Boy: A Memoir. New York: HarperCollins, 2001.

The Journal of Biddy Owens: The Negro Leagues, Birmingham, Alabama, 1948. (My Name Is America: A Dear America Book). New York: Scholastic, 2001.

145th Street: Short Stories. New York: Delacorte, 2000.

The Blues of Flats Brown. Illustrated by Nina Laden. New York: Holiday House, 2000.

The Greatest: The Life of Muhammad Ali. New York: Scholastic, 2000.

Malcolm X: A Fire Burning Brightly. Illustrated by Leonard Jenkins. New York: HarperCollins, 2000.

At Her Majesty's Request: An African Princess in Victorian England. New York: Scholastic, 1999.

The Journal of Joshua Loper: A Black Cowboy: Chisholm Trail, 1871. (My Name Is America: A Dear America Book). New York: Scholastic, 1999.

The Journal of Scott Pendleton Collins: World War II Soldier: Normandy, France, 1944. (My Name Is America: A Dear America Book). New York: Scholastic, 1999.

Monster. New York: HarperCollins, 1999.

Angel to Angel: A Mother's Gift of Love. New York: HarperCollins, 1998.

Slam! New York: Scholastic, 1998.

Amistad: A Long Road to Freedom. New York: Dutton, 1997.

Harlem. Illustrated by Christopher Myers. New York: Scholastic, 1997.

How Mr. Monkey Saw the Whole World. Illustrated by Synthia Saint James. New York: Doubleday, 1996.

One More River to Cross: An African American Photograph Album. New York: Harcourt Brace, 1996.

Smiffy Blue, Ace Crime Detective: Case of the Missing Ruby and Other Stories. New York: Scholastic, 1996.

Toussaint L'Ouverture: The Fight for Haiti's Freedom. Illustrations by Jacob Lawrence. New York: Simon & Schuster, 1996.

The Dragon Takes a Wife. Illustrated by Fiona French. New York: Scholastic, 1995. Earlier edition: Illustrated by Ann Grifalconi. Indianapolis: Bobbs-Merrill, 1972.

Glorious Angels: A Celebration of Children. New York: HarperCollins, 1995.

Shadow of the Red Moon. Illustrated by Christopher Myers. New York: Scholastic, 1995.

The Story of the Three Kingdoms. Illustrated by Ashley Bryan. New York: HarperCollins, 1995.

Darnell Rock Reporting. New York: Delacorte, 1994.

The Glory Field. New York: Scholastic, 1994.

Brown Angels: An Album of Pictures and Verse. New York: HarperCollins, 1993.

Malcolm X: By Any Means Necessary. New York: Scholastic, 1993.

A Place Called Heartbreak: A Story of Vietnam. Austin, TX: Raintree Steck-Vaughn, 1993.

Young Martin's Promise. Austin, TX: Raintree Steck-Vaughn, 1993.

Mop, Moondance, and the Nagasaki Knights. New York: Delacorte, 1992.

The Righteous Revenge of Artemis Bonner. New York: HarperCollins, 1992.

Somewhere in the Darkness. New York: Scholastic, 1992.

Now Is Your Time!: The African-American Struggle for Freedom. New York: HarperCollins, 1991.

The Mouse Rap. New York: HarperCollins, 1990.

Fallen Angels. New York: Scholastic, 1988.

Me, Mop, and the Moondance Kid. New York: Delacorte, 1988.

Scorpions. New York: HarperCollins, 1988.

Crystal. New York: Viking, 1987.

Ambush in the Amazon. (Arrow Series). New York: Viking, 1986.

Duel in the Desert. (Arrow Series). New York: Viking, 1986.

Sweet Illusions. New York: Teachers & Writers Collaborative, 1986.

Adventure in Granada. (Arrow Series). New York: Viking, 1985.

The Hidden Shrine. (Arrow Series). New York: Viking, 1985.

Motown and Didi. New York: Viking, 1984.

The Outside Shot. New York: Delacorte, 1984.

The Nicholas Factor. New York: Viking, 1983.

Tales of a Dead King. New York: William Morrow, 1983.

Won't Know Till I Get There. New York: Viking, 1982.

Hoops. New York: Delacorte, 1981.

The Legend of Tarik. New York: Viking, 1981.

The Black Pearl and the Ghost; Or, One Mystery after Another. Illustrated by Robert Quackenbush. New York: Viking, 1980.

The Golden Serpent. Illustrated by Alice and Martin Provensen. New York: Viking, 1980.

The Young Landlords. New York: Viking, 1979.

It Ain't All for Nothin'. New York: Viking, 1978; reprint: New York: HarperCollins, 2003.

Brainstorm. Illustrated with photographs by Charles Freedman. New York: Franklin Watts, 1977.

Mojo and the Russians. New York: Viking, 1977.

Victory for Jamie. New York: Scholastic, 1977.

Social Welfare: A First Book. New York: Franklin Watts, 1976.

Fast Sam, Cool Clyde, and Stuff. New York: Viking, 1975.

The World of Work: A Guide to Choosing a Career. Indianapolis: Bobbs-Merrill, 1975.

Fly, Jimmy, Fly! Illustrated by Moneta Barnett. New York: Putnam, 1974.

The Dancers. Illustrated by Anne Rockwell. New York: Parents Magazine Press, 1972.

Where Does the Day Go? Illustrated by Leo Carty. New York: Parents Magazine Press, 1969.

The Party. (Writing as Stacie Johnson). (18 Pine Street Series). New York: Delacorte, 1993.

The Prince. (Writing as Stacie Johnson). (18 Pine Street Series). New York: Delacorte, 1993.

Sort of Sisters. (Writing as Stacie Johnson). New York: Delacorte, 1993.